MIRRORS, MICE, & MUSTACHES

*A Sampling of Superstitions
& Popular Beliefs in Texas*

George D. Hendricks

SOUTHERN METHODIST UNIVERSITY PRESS

Dallas

© 1966 by Texas Folklore Society
Third Printing 1981

Library of Congress Cataloging in Publication Data
Hendricks, George David. 1913-
　Mirrors, mice & mustaches.

　Reprint of the ed. published by the Texas Folklore Society, Austin, as no. 1 of Paisano books.
　Includes bibliographical references and index.
　1. Folk-lore—Texas.　I. Title.
GR110.T5H4　1980　　　398'.3'09764　　　80-27405
ISBN 0-87074-075-X

TO PEGGY

INTRODUCTION

Some superstitions and popular beliefs are based upon the profoundest human motivations. We pick up a horseshoe and nail it over the door for luck, but inquiry has shown that the horseshoe is a feminine sexual symbol and that virtually every culture the world over from the beginning of time has worshiped the goddess of fertility represented by that symbol. Three days of the week—Sunday, Monday, and Friday—were named for fertility gods; and there is more to this subject than we have space here to elucidate.[1]

Deeply entrenched into the human character is the consideration as to whether we should look back or not, either in a physical or chronological sense. This involves a multitude of popular beliefs and superstitions mirrored in proverbs, legends, rituals, and folktales both informal and literary, both ancient and modern.[2] Coleridge knew that behind the seaman's superstition (which still exists) against killing a bird of good omen lay a universal human scruple against interfering with nature's balance or a useless exploitation of natural resources. He knew also the tragic results of such indiscretion. Scholars like Sir James George Frazer and Philip Waterman have found that mistletoe is efficacious as a fertility symbol, cure-all for man and beast, aphrodisiac, agent of invulnerability, and counteragent against witches and conjurers, all because of a folk conception of the very nature of life.

Profoundly serious human actions resulting from an admixture of Christianity and paganism can deteriorate into superficiality. I don't remember where I read that there were thirteen people at Christ's last supper, that he was crucified on a Friday, that enroute up Calvary hill as he bore his cross some grateful but fearful witnesses quietly knocked on the wood of the cross to indicate their appreciation for his sacrifice, and that the triangle is a symbol of the Holy Trinity. Hence, Friday the thirteenth is unlucky, to knock on wood is to be grateful, and to walk under a ladder is to break the sign of a triangle and hence to render asunder the Trinity—I suppose a symbol of trespass. I also have a theory about the number seven, which anybody knows is endlessly recurrent in folk luck motifs. It is the sum of four and three, of all things terrestrial (four cardinal directions on this good earth) and of all things celestial (the Trinity). It encompasses all good things in this life and in the next, all things tangible and intangible. Why shouldn't it be lucky?

With some degree of primitive logic the human being makes analogous associations resulting in what Frazer would call homeopathic magic. In other words, like produces like. A student from the Rio Grande Valley told me that while she was pregnant her primitive friends told her to walk barefooted between corn rows. It would help her, and it would help the corn. Both were about to bear. Rain has been a symbol of sorrowful tears in both folk and formal literature. Man is as he is because the weather is as it is. The number of raindrops that fall during a bride's wedding will be the number of teardrops she will shed the rest of her life, we are told. To break a mirror brings on seven years of bad luck. In breaking your image you are destroying the "other" you (losing your soul). And in Texas red-headed farmers grow better, hotter pepper plants than blonds or brunets. Then there is contagious magic. The mere touching of an object, or even the proximity of it, produces direct and related results. You catch warts from frogs because they have skins that look warty. You get rid of a wart by sticking a pin in it till it bleeds, then sticking the same pin into a corn kernel, and burying it in the ground. As it germinates, so will your wart grow out of your skin. You get rid of an undesirable man by nailing his shoe sole to a freight car. The farther away the car goes, the farther away he will go.

We must admit that some folk beliefs are based upon natural

phenomena. Roy Bedichek has shown that science has sometimes had to take a back seat to folklore. There really is such a thing as a dying swan song, and birds really do hibernate.[3] These are not idle inventions of the fertile folk imagination; what the scientists once scoffed at, they now accept as fact. People say it will rain within the same number of days as there are stars within the circle around a moon. The size of the circle probably depends upon the humidity and the visibility of the atmosphere, and there ought to be a relationship to the likelihood of rain.

We cannot deny, also, that we must accept some popular aphoristic folk beliefs as being perfectly true, according to either their surface meaning or their figurative ramifications. A person, it is said, will never go broke if he always keeps a half dollar coin in his pocket. How *could* he? If a person creeps on his hands and knees three times from east to west through a bramble hedge, his blackheads will all disappear. Of course they will, and so will his skin with them. A person can cure himself of the hives if he will walk backwards blindfolded three times around a persimmon tree and *not* think of an opossum. To me, this test is impossible in the first place; so the statement *must* be true.

These latter examples border upon another type of entry, which to me is not really a belief or superstition. It is, frankly, a mere practical joke designed as a popular belief. If you bite the head off a butterfly, you will get a new dress the same color as that of the butterfly (again, like produces like). To cure a child's swollen gums in teething, the mother should bite the head off a live mouse. Can you imagine the sadistic pleasure of the practical joker enjoying the expression on the face of either the girl desirous of a new dress or the anxious mother? If a boy wants his girl to be "nice," he should nail a bottle of My Sin perfume hanging from a three-foot string from the thirteenth branch from the top of a pecan tree. Visualize the delight of the practical jokester watching his ludicrous gullible victim climbing a tree. In this case the jokester has an "out" if the trick doesn't "work." He can always say that this works only on Friday before 8 p.m.

Still others are not practical jokes, but they are kindred. Some are designed to coerce children into coöperation and good behavior. It is bad luck to leave hats or shoes on top of a bed or table. If you eat the very last biscuit, you will be an old maid. If you sweep under a person's feet, she will never marry. To carry a hoe or rake through the house is bad luck. To whistle at the table is bad luck.

Other superstitions or misconceptions sometimes developing into widespread beliefs come from the attempt of the uneducated or inexperienced to explain what they do not understand and what they fear in nature. This can easily be illustrated with a quick glance at the medieval bestiary. Or a modicum of research into current ideas of natural history will suffice. Lloyd Jeffrey's interpretation of snake yarns about the West and Southwest reveals, for example, why a person might believe that a mother snake swallows her young.[4] My own research concerning pioneers' reactions to wild animals in the West revealed popular misconceptions and superstitions because of their lack of familiarity with the species.[5]

But there are plentiful entries in this book, as there are in any such collection, that I do not profess to be able to explain. I am not a professional psychologist, but it does not take a trained expert to make the observations in the preceding paragraphs. It seems to me that they are based on plain common sense. If there are any other explanations, anybody's guess is as good as mine.

This book does not need a lengthy introduction. A short explanation is in order. Professor Wayland D. Hand of the University of California at Los Angeles has a Guggenheim grant to publish a multi-volume, definitive edition of American popular beliefs and superstitions. He has solicited me to make a collection from Texas and twenty-nine others all over the country to do the same for their respective areas. To date I have over 6,000 cards from all over the state. When all the collections are finished, Professor Hand will assimilate them for his publication.

My collection came from all over Texas. I am indebted to my on-campus colleagues and students at North Texas State University, to my ex-students, to members of the Texas Folklore Society, to certain members of the Texas press and their reading public, and to certain officials and classroom teachers in various Texas public schools. Roughly sixty per cent of the collection came from this latter source. I would like particularly to acknowledge the work (not to the exclusion of others) of such people as Irene Seidensticker of San Antonio, Jean Dugat of Beeville, Mrs. Vivian Hyer of Center,

INTRODUCTION

Mrs. Bernice L. Harris of Lufkin, Mrs. Ottis Cash of Knox City, Mrs. T. A. Carmichael of Port Lavaca, J. W. Nixon of Laredo, and Herman Sullivan of Carrizo Springs—all public school people. Also, Professor Roger Abrahams of the University of Texas and his students like Barbara Ann Simota and David B. Gracy, and Professor John West of Texas Western and his students like Margaret Divelbiss and Janet Irvin. Also, James L. Rogers, Administrative Vice President of North Texas State and former News Service Director; members of the Associated Press and the United Press International; and George Fuermann of the *Houston Post*. Also, non-academic members of the Texas Folklore Society such as John Ben Sheppard and Stanley Marcus. Also, Texas citizens such as H. D. Odum, a rural mail carrier from Whitesboro who happened to notice something about the collection in a newspaper and took it upon himself to stop at every house on his route to make his own collection of authentic rural folk-beliefs.

For the purpose of this particular book, I intentionally picked out from the total collection of over 6,000 items only those which to my knowledge have not yet appeared in print in Texas and those which seemed to be of most interest.[6] Two other things need explaining. After each item two names are usually given, the first specifying the informant and the second the collector. When only one name is given, it belongs to the informant and I am the collector myself. The informant does not necessarily believe the entry but he knows someone who does. And I know you may be wondering about the title of the book. Somewhere inside you will find superstitions or popular beliefs pertaining to mirrors, to mice, and to mustaches. The title suggests the wide range of things about which the folk mind can be superstitious, to which it attaches picturesque beliefs.

I am indebted to the North Texas State University Faculty Research Council for the grants which enabled me to make the collection from which these samples have been taken. I am further indebted to the Texas Folklore Society for making this publication possible.

GEORGE D. HENDRICKS
Denton, Texas
July 4, 1965

[1] "Why Is the Horseshoe Lucky?" *Pennsylvania Archaeologist,* XXIX (1959), pp. 66–72.

[2] "Don't Look Back," in *Singers and Storytellers* (Dallas, 1961), pp. 69–75. ("Publications of the Texas Folklore Society," XXX.)

[3] Roy Bedichek, "Folklore in Natural History," in *Folk Travelers* (Dallas, 1953), pp. 18–39. ("Publications of the Texas Folklore Society," XXV.)

[4] Lloyd N. Jeffrey, "Snake Yarns of the West and Southwest," *Western Folklore,* XIV (1955), pp. 246–58.

[5] "Misconceptions Concerning Western Wild Animals," *Western Folklore,* XII (1953), pp. 119–27.

[6] In addition to the articles cited above, there are three others that have to do with Texas superstitions. 1. Frost Woodhull, "Ranch *Remedios,*" in *Man, Bird, and Beast* (Austin, 1930), pp. 9–73. ("Publications of the Texas Folklore Society," VIII.) 2. Tressa Turner, "The Human Comedy in Folk Superstitutions," in *Straight Texas* (Austin, 1937), pp. 146–75. ("Publications of the Texas Folklore Society," XIII.) 3. George D. Hendricks, "Superstitions Collected in Denton, Texas," *Western Folklore,* XV (1956), pp. 1–18.

CONTENTS

Animals	3
Birth, Infancy, Childhood	7
Love, Courtship, Marriage	11
Dreams and Wishes	17
Death and Burial	23
Human Body, Folk Medicine	31
Numbers, Seasons, Times of Day	57
Trades and Professions	61
Sports	62
Weather	66
Miscellaneous	72
Index	97

MIRRORS, MICE, & MUSTACHES

ANIMALS

Adder

If you hang an adder's skin in the rafters, your house will never catch fire.

> Rickey Wilborn, Port Lavaca
> Mrs. T. A. Carmichael, Port Lavaca

Ant

If you are standing in an ant pile, close your eyes and bite your tongue as hard as possible, and they won't bite you.

> Norma Guana, San Antonio
> Irene Seidensticker, San Antonio

Put bluing on red ant bites. This does not work for black ant bites.

> Mrs. N. J. Nelson, El Paso
> Janet Irvin, El Paso

Armadillo

There is but one way you can pull an armadillo out of a hole. First, let him calm down a bit, then gently slip your hand into the hole, and try to scratch his tummy. This will relax him, and if you jerk quickly, you will pull him out.

> J. C. Caraway, Decatur
> Brent Cody Barron, Irving

Bull

If you breed a young bull to an old cow, it will ruin the bull.

> Roger Vassar, Knox City
> Mrs. Ottis Cash, Knox City

Calf

If you cut the tails off your cows and bulls, all the calves will be bobtailed.
>Roger Vassar, Knox City
>Mrs. Ottis Cash, Knox City

Cat

Company will come from the direction a cat's tail points when the cat is washing his face.
>Kay Lynne Busbee, Comfort
>Neil Hawkins, Denton

Chicken

Smoke from a fire made out of chicken feathers is a good disinfectant.
>Mrs. C. Spearman, El Paso
>Janet Irvin, El Paso

Cow

If you stir your milk with a fork, the cow will go dry.
>Dr. Robert J. Robinson, Galveston
>George Fuermann, Houston

Dog

If dogs breed in the morning, there will be more males than females.
>Mrs. Ralph T. Caldwell, Lubbock

If a dog is bitten by a peccary, after the peccary is killed put some blood from the peccary on the dog's wound so he will not continue to bleed and be cured generally.
>Cayetano J. De LaGarza, Laredo
>J. W. Nixon, Laredo

Pekinese dogs cause cancer.

> Mrs. D. L. Pickens, El Paso
> Alma P. Miller, El Paso

Quiet a howling, mournful dog at night by turning a shoe upside down.

> Diana Alanis, San Juan
> T. M. Harwell, Edinburg

To terrify a charging dog, bend over frontwards and look at him from between your knees, backside toward the dog.

> Howard C. Key, Denton

If you get a dog that won't stay home, cut the tip of his tail off and bury it under your back door step. Then he'll never leave.

> Mr. and Mrs. R. W. Fults, Center
> Jerry Fults, Center

If you get up and cross your shoes, the dogs will stop barking.

> Herman Sullivan, Carrizo Springs

Fish

In Texas some people carry a small bone from a fish's head as a charm against evil. This charm is most effective after it has been lost.

> Chris Webb, Lubbock
> Mrs. Ted Pinkston, Lubbock

Grasshopper

If you catch a grasshopper and bite his head off, you'll find some money.

> Judi McDuff, Dallas

Horned Toad

Stepping on a horned toad will cause a bump which in turn will cause a sore which will not heal. Eventually this gets worse until the foot rots away.

> Jimmy Martinez, Austin
> Barbara Ann Simota, Austin

Horse

A horse with four white feet, keep him not a day.
A horse with three white feet, send him far away.
A horse with two white feet, give him to a friend.
A horse with one white foot, keep him till the end.

> Price Wooldridge, Lubbock
> Mrs. Ralph T. Caldwell, Lubbock

Jaybirds

The jaybirds go down to the devil's house every Friday to tell all the bad things that have happened during the week. You seldom see a jaybird on Friday. The few that do not go remain to keep check on what people do.

> E. L. Yeats, Roby

Lizard

If you kill a lizard or a frog, it will come again at night and choke you.

> Herman Sullivan, Carrizo Springs

Owl

To stop an owl at night, pull the tongue out of a shoe and set it under the bed.

> Mrs. Hubert C. Lyon, Terrell
> Mrs. Eugene Butler, Dallas

If you want an owl to stop screeching, turn your pocket inside out and twist it. This action breaks the owl's neck.

> Gary Clemmons, Lubbock
> Peggy Johnson, Lubbock

Rabbit

Do not depend on a rabbit's foot,
Nor get your hopes up soon,
Unless it is the left hind one
And was caught by the light of the moon.

> Mrs. Julius Schwartz, Schulenburg
> George Fuermann, Houston

Rat

If you have rats in your house, take two of them and tie their tails together and all the rats will leave. Sprinkle them with sugar, or the house will disappear, too.

> Joyce Ann Williams, Dallas
> Constance Elaine Davis, Dallas

Snake

If you see the trail of a snake and don't erase it, the angels won't be with you and protect you.

> Herman Sullivan, Carrizo Springs

BIRTH, INFANCY, CHILDHOOD

Baby

After the birth of a baby, a mother must abstain from all acidic foods (oranges, lemons, etc.); otherwise she will not conceive again.

> Maria Gomez, San Antonio
> Gordon Sutton, San Antonio

When a baby drinks out of a bottle instead of nursing his mother, he will be hard-headed.

> Mrs. Peggy Mayes, Rock Springs
> Mrs. Regina Koeniger, Fort Worth

If a man hangs his trousers on the bedpost, his wife will have a baby.

> Esther Tribble, Dallas
> Robert Tribble, Dallas

If a woman wears high heels while she is pregnant, her baby will be cross-eyed.

> Nancy Bryant, Tyler

Birth Pains

During the birth of a child, you must put a knife under the bed of the mother in order to cut the pains.

> Mrs. Lois Sutherland, Austin
> Anne H. Sutherland, Austin

Child

If you want your child to rise in the world, carry it upstairs when it is one day old.

> Sherry Eckert, Lubbock
> Mrs. Ralph T. Caldwell, Lubbock

To cure cowardice in children, rip the heart from a live hawk and make them eat it.

> J. Pecorino, Kemah

Children should not eat mustard, because it makes their feet stink.

> Mrs. De La Cruz, Austin
> Barbara Ann Simota, Austin

Defect

If a pregnant woman sees a person with a defect and says something about the person, the baby will be born with the same defect.

> Rose Marie Lopez, San Antonio
> Mrs. Esther Fletcher, San Antonio

Eclipse

If an expectant mother wishes to go outside her home on a night when there is a total eclipse of the moon, she must wear a key hanging from a string around her neck or the child will be born deformed.

> Mrs. Louis Scott, San Antonio
> Octavio A. Trevino, San Antonio

Fingernails

If you cut your baby's fingernails while he is still young, this could cause the child to steal when he gets older.

> Willie Stoker, El Paso
> John Jimerson, El Paso

Hair

If a child gets his hair cut before he is one year old, he will stutter.

> Lucille Carlisle, El Paso
> John Jimerson, El Paso

Head

If you rub a baby's head with a silk handkerchief, it will have curly hair.

> Mrs. W. C. Cason, Van Alstyne

Intelligence

Children who are specially intelligent are likely to be retarded or weak physically.

Alma Diaz, Austin
Barbara Ann Simota, Austin

Knife

Place a knife under the mattress when in child labor to cut the pain.

Suzie Smith, Denton
Judy L. Branham, Fort Worth

Moon

Most good children are born with the moon is full.

Dianna L. Scoggins, Longview

Navel

If a baby's navel protrudes, bury a hen egg on the southeast corner of the house with a little part of the egg out of the ground. When the egg rots, the navel will go down.

Olive Jane Strange, Temple
Margaret Gresham, Temple

Nose

If your nose runs and your feet smell, you were born upside down.

Mrs. Charles Hillman, Sherman
Jeanne Caldwell, Russell

Pregnancy

If you eat cucumbers while pregnant, you will miscarry.

Mrs. Felix Jones, Odessa
Mrs. J. M. Defee, Odessa

If a pregnant woman hangs clothes on a line above her head, the unborn child will be strangled on the umbilical cord.

Helen Hanicak, Denton

Veil

If a baby is born with a veil over its face, he is supposed to be incapable of drowning and able to predict deaths.

Margaret Layton, Galveston

LOVE, COURTSHIP, MARRIAGE

Bedroom

Name the four corners of your bedroom with your lovers' names. The first corner you look at in the morning will show the one you are to wed.

Miss Alice Stevens, Austin

Bride

If a bride hears a cat sneeze the day before her wedding, her married life will be happy.

Vicki Henley, Gainesville
Don Pope, Gainesville

Buzzard

When you see a buzzard, count how many times he flaps his wings until he is out of sight. If he flaps them a lot your sweetheart loves you a lot; but if he doesn't flap them, he doesn't love you.

Meg Gault, Center
Mrs. Vivian Hyer, Center

Convertibles

Count red convertibles with boys driving. The hundredth car contains the boy you will marry.

Sandra Rosenfield, El Paso
Dorothy English, El Paso

Drunkard

If you get your apron wet while doing the laundry, it is a sign that you will marry a drunkard.

       Mrs. La Rue Odom, Whitesboro
       H. D. Odom, Whitesboro

Female Companion

Bad luck will come to any man who sits before his female companion is seated, unless she walks in and out of the door three times, and returns to a different seat in the room. During the last entrance the man must stand and remain standing until the woman is seated.

       Sandra Sutherland, San Antonio
       Irene Seidensticker, San Antonio

Frying Pan

If a girl eats from a frying pan, it will rain on her wedding.

       Mary Alice Blyth, San Antonio
       Irene Seidensticker, San Antonio

Graveyard

If you don't hold your breath when passing by a graveyard, you'll lose your true love.

       Jan Sutton, Knox City
       Mrs. Ottis Cash, Knox City

Hair

If you want a girl to love you, get her signature on a piece of paper, and wrap a small lock of her hair in this paper. Sign your name and put a small lock of your hair in this bundle also. Put this little bundle in a pot of boiling water with sugar and allow to cool for 24 hours.

       Howard Hanks, Jr., Denton

Halloween

If you back down the basement steps on Halloween, holding a mirror over your shoulder, and a lighted candle in your hand, you'll see the face of the one you'll marry in the mirror.

>Mary Jane Thompson, El Paso
>Mary Ann Thompson, El Paso

Handkerchief

On the evening before May Day if you place a white handkerchief on the blades of wheat in a wheat field, the initials of the one you'll marry will appear in green on the handkerchief the next day.

>Kay Susott, Waco
>Danny Susott, Waco

If a handkerchief is wetted and hung out the window, the wrinkles will form your true love's name.

>Margaret Dervier, San Antonio
>Frank Heintzen, San Antonio

Heart

If you swallow the heart of a chicken in one piece you will marry your boyfriend.

>Lucy B. Hill, San Antonio
>Mrs. Mary Jo Galbraith, San Antonio

Husband

Never iron the tail of your husband's shirt first or he'll come to hate you.

>Verna M. Thompson, Houston
>George Fuermann, Houston

Initial Letter

When you get married, the initial letter of your maiden name should not be the initial letter of your new name. This is expressed in a rhyme:
Change the name and not the letter,
Change for worse and not for better!

>Mrs. Lula Glass, Zephyr
>Laverne Keeler Kilgore, Sherman

Kiss

You reveal the way you kiss by the position of your mouth while drinking from a bottle.

>Susan Hayes Long, Denton

Knife

While you're working in the kitchen and a knife drops out of your hand, it's a sure sign you will quarrel with your husband.

>Mrs. John Emmett, Dallas
>David Emmett, Denton

Marriage

After a girl stamps (counts by sticking her finger in her mouth and striking her palm) twenty-five couples holding hands, fifty boys on bikes, and one hundred Cadillacs, the next boy she sees will be the one she will marry.

>Betty English, El Paso
>Dorothy English, El Paso

May First

Look down into the well on May first to see the man you will marry.

>Mrs. Lucinda Owen, Athens
>Mrs. Eva Coleman, Denton

Meal

A girl should never take the last piece of bread at a meal. To do so will cause her to be an old maid.

> Patricia Pope, Gainesville

Mirror

If a bride looks at herself in a mirror after she has dressed for her wedding, she and her husband-to-be will have a quarrel.

> Carrie Sherwood, San Antonio
> Jack Thrasher, San Antonio

Pear Tree

If a maiden sees a pear tree on Christmas Eve when the moon is full, and if she walks around it three times backwards, her husband-to-be will appear in an image.

> Patricia Gallatin, Denton

Pendant

If a girl has a pendant, or drop on a chain around her neck, and the clasp touches the pendant or drop, she should kiss the chain and turn the clasp back around, so that her boyfriend will think about her.

> Judith Ann Cole, Dallas
> Jim Edwards, Denton

Shoe

If you bury one of your husband's worn-out shoes under the doorstep, he will never step out on you.

> Alice Katherine Mosier, Dallas
> Shirley Dean Mosier, Dallas

Singing

If you sing at the table, you will have a crazy husband.

>Donna Lee, Brownwood
>Sue Fuller, Waxahachie

Spider

If you have a spider on your wedding dress, you will have good luck.

>Sue Douglas, Austin
>Larry Taylor, Dallas

Sweeping

If you sweep at night, you will lose your husband.

>Herman Sullivan, Carrizo Springs

Sweetheart

To get your boyfriend back from his new sweetheart, write their names on a strip of paper, wrap it around an apple, and place it under her house. As the apple withers, so will his love for her.

>Ellen Welling, Fort Worth

Wedding

If four people cross one another's hands when they shake hands, there will be a wedding.

>Mrs. D. H. Dean, Jr., Dallas
>Dell Webb, Dallas

Wedding Dress

If you try on somebody else's wedding dress once, you will never get married.

>Santos Cavazos, San Benito
>Maria Leal, San Benito

Wedding Ring

If you wear another person's wedding ring, you'll have an unhappy life.

Herman Sullivan, Carrizo Springs

Well

Walk away from a well nine feet, then back up to the well nine feet. Look down into the well nine feet, and you will see the man you are to marry.

Mrs. Myrie Jackson, Lufkin
Mrs. Bernice L. Harris, Lufkin

Window

If you climb in and out a window, you'll get a dumb husband.

Mrs. Warren Kinstlery, Denton
Richard Earnhart, Denton

DREAMS AND WISHES

Animals

Deviate behavior will occur in your family if you dream of animals, especially a great number of animals.

Boyd Shepherd, Denton
Miss Fleur Fuller, Denton

Bed

Whatever you dream the first night in a new bed or a new house will come true.

Sharon Evans, Denton

Bottles

It's bad luck (usually a death warning) if you hear bottles rolling down a stairway and breaking upon reaching the floor and if there is no broken glass when you look for it.

Jim Davis, Grapevine
Larry Banks, Grapevine

Bridge

If you hold your breath while crossing a short, straight bridge, your wish will come true.

>Jerry Fults, Center
>Mrs. Vivian Hyer, Center

Bridge Game

In bridge when the ace, two, three, and four of a suit are played in one trick, the cards must be turned face down and shuffled. Each player draws a card, and the one with the ace makes a wish that will come true.

>Mrs. R. A. Northington, Fort Worth
>Sheila Tomlin, Fort Worth

Butterfly

Eat a butterfly head, and you will get a dress the color of the butterfly.

>Almarie Chilton, Athens
>A. C. Norman, Athens

Button

If you find a button and put it in your shoe, you will have a date before the day is over.

>Robert Shannon Astor, Brownwood
>Mrs. Vanita Martin, Brownwood

Car

If you see a car with only one light, touch the roof of the car and say a magic word, "Padoodalie," and make a wish. In an alternate version, young people, instead of wishing, substitute kissing on a date.

>Julie Miller, El Paso
>Dorothy English, El Paso

Cliff

If you dream you are falling off a cliff and you hit the bottom, you will die the next day.

> Steve Miller, Mesquite
> Kenneth Pepper, Dallas

Cross

It's good luck to carry a Virginia Fairy Cross (staurolite crystal). Indian tears at the time of Christ's crucifixion were turned to these stones.

> Jan Esslinger, Dallas
> Larry Banks, Grapevine

Dress

If one hem of your dress gets turned up, kiss it before turning it down, and make a wish. The wish will come true.

> Vallie Mae Schiling, Beeville
> Jean Dugat, Beeville

Eggs

If you dream about eggs, someone is going to tell lies about you.

> Dominga Ybarra, Port Lavaca
> Mrs. T. A. Carmichael, Port Lavaca

Dream of eggs and you will quarrel with a friend.

> Sherry Eckert, Lubbock
> Mrs. Ralph T. Caldwell, Lubbock

Eyelashes

When a person sees one of your eyelashes fallen from the lid of eye, he may tell you to make a wish and to guess which side of your face the eyelash is on. If you guess correctly, your wish will come true.

> Susan Hayes Long, Denton

Fingers

Pop you ten fingers and make a wish, and it will come true.

Herman Sullivan, Carizzo Springs

Fish

If you dream of fish, it is the sign that a baby is being born.

Mrs. E. T. Sorrells, Dallas
Anita Low, Dallas

Graveyard

If you go in the graveyard on a dark night, and stick a fork in a grave while wishing you will marry a rich man, you will marry a rich man.

Mrs. Myrie Jackson, Lufkin
Mrs. Bernice L. Harris, Lufkin

Gum

When taking gum from a freshly opened pack, choose the middle stick. Make a wish and name a time for throwing the gum away. If you throw out the gum at this time, your wish will come true.

Jo Ann Boyd, Denton

Horses

When taking a trip, count the white horses (each counts 1), and the white mules (each counts 10). When you reach 100, make a wish and it will come true.

Mrs. Jewell Silber, San Antonio

Lion

If you dream of a lion, your Prince Charming will come.

Miss Elida Cantu, San Antonio
Mary H. Zehr, San Antonio

Money

Many years ago, a twelve-inch pipe gushed water out of the ground east of Gordonville, Texas. People used to make wishes and drop money into the pipe. There is no telling how much money was dropped into the old well, whose crystal clear water gushed out and formed a lake behind it. Flowing Wells, as this spot used to be called, now lies at the bottom of Lake Texoma across from Big Joe's Fishing Camp. If old memories could speak, many a tale would come from its depths.

Mrs. W. L. McDonnold, Sadler
H. D. Odom, Whitesboro

Moon

Turn a piece of silver in your pocket on seeing a new or full moon if you want your wish to come true.

Jerry Fults, Center
Mrs. Vivian Hyer, Center

Mountain

If you dream that you are falling off a mountain, the next day you will have bad luck.

Jimmie Ritchie, Dallas
Steve Miller, Mesquite

Pie

If you cut the front triangle of a piece of pie and put it aside and eat it last, you will get your first wish.

Georgia Atkinson Funston, Fort Worth

Shoes

Turn your shoes upside down under the bed at night, and you won't have bad dreams.

Mary Simmons, Fort Worth
Fleur Fuller, Denton

If you want to dream about everything that will happen to you the next day, put your shoes into your hat, and set the hat under the foot of your bed before you go to bed.

Snakes

Herman Sullivan, Carrizo Springs

Dreaming of snakes and/or muddy water is forewarning of bad luck.

Clayton Hamilton, Clint
Mary Ann Thompson, El Paso

If you dream of snakes at night, you will make an enemy the next day.

Jon Payne, Edna
Grace Wellborn, Lubbock

Toe

If a person stumps his toe in the daytime, he will have bad dreams at night.

George A. Strickland, San Antonio
Irene Seidensticker, San Antonio

Walking

When you dream that you are walking in mud, it means that you are going to become ill.

Herman Sullivan, Carrizo Springs

Water

If you dream about water, it means tears the next day.

Alvin P. Mitchell, Temple
David R. Soto, Temple

Whiskey

Dreams about a member of your family that picture this person as getting hurt will not come true if you have him swallow a raw egg with the aid of a jigger of whiskey and then count to ten backwards slowly.

                Howard Hanks, Denton

DEATH AND BURIAL

Bird

If a bird tries to enter the house, one of the family is going to die.

                Janet Pennycuick, San Antonio
                Gale Nelson, San Antonio

If a bird flies down the chimney, someone in the family will soon die.

                Mrs. Elizabeth Crabtree, Arlington
                Frances Ward, Arlington

Black Pepper

Black pepper on fish kills you.

                Mrs. Lemwell East, Travis
                Mrs. Maura Darrouzet, Austin

Blood

If someone is killed in a house and the blood is cleaned up, every time it rains the blood will come back.

                Hugh Lamar Amboree, Wharton
                Frances T. Masterson, Wharton

Butterfly

When a black butterfly enters into your home, this indicates that someone will die.

                Ruth Veronica Yates, San Antonio
                John Igo, San Antonio

Buzzard

If a buzzard's shadow crosses over you, you will die.

      Mrs. Rufus King, Gonzales
      Chris Werner, Austin

Cat

If a black cat meows on your porch or under your window, there will be a death in the famiy.

      Mrs. Felix R. McCoy, Fort Worth
      Mary McCoy, Denton

Clothes

If you travel with wet clothes, you will come to a sudden death.

      Mrs. Louise Wilson, Dallas
      Walter L. Busby, Dallas

Crawl

If a person is lying down and you crawl over him, one of your friends will die.

      Dominga Ybarra, Port Lavaca
      Mrs. T. A. Carmichael, Port Lavaca

Dead

If you feel that your home is being visited by the dead, nine different verses of the Psalms should be placed in nine different places throughout the house to bring peace of mind.

      Mrs. Lucille Carlisle, El Paso
      John Jimerson, El Paso

Debt

If a man dies owing a debt, his soul will not rest until the next of kin pays it.

      Mrs. Livia Diaz, Austin
      Barbara Ann Simota, Austin

Dog

If the family dog crawls on his stomach, someone in the family will die that year. It will be the first person whom the dog looks at after he gets up from crawling on his stomach.

> Mrs. Janie Boone, Lufkin
> Mrs. Bernice L. Harris, Lufkin

If a dog turns over with this feet in the air, he's measuring his owner's grave.

> Mrs. Lemwell East, Austin
> Mrs. Maura Darrouzet, Austin

Door

If you build a new door in a house while remodeling, a corpse will be carried out of the house through that door within a year's time.

> Mrs. J. W. Ford, Corsicana
> Jean Dugat, Beeville

Drown

A person who is tattooed will never drown at sea, nor will he ever be bothered by sharks.

> Robert Tribble, Dallas

East

The body must be placed in the grave with the face facing the east or the rising sun.

> H. D. Odom, Whitesboro

Evil Eye

One who is not cured of Mal de Ojo (evil eye) will die as a result of the rupture of his gall bladder and the spread of the bile through his body.

> Gregorio Bustamante, Mercedes
> Baldemar Zuniga, Mercedes

Fish

Don't eat fish after you have a baby, or you'll die.

        Mrs. Lemwell East, Austin
        Mrs. Maura Darrouzet, Austin

Funeral

Some Mexicans feel that on the day of a funeral all mirrors in the house should be taken down or turned around.

        Mrs. Walter Sparks, Jr., Portland
        Gail Mayo, Taft

It is bad luck to change the time of a funeral.

        Alice Stevens, Austin

It is bad luck to be the last to leave the cemetery after a funeral.

        Linda Mullins, Lubbock
        Mrs. Ted Pinkston, Lubbock

If you count the cars in a funeral procession, that is the number of days you have left to live.

        Mary Jane Perez, Bay City

Ghost

There is a story about a young girl who appears at White Rock Lake in Dallas, wet and alone. She is taken to an apartment by an unsuspecting person and then disappears. This has supposedly happened several times. People have driven around the lake at night and have seen the girl in a wet white dress. She asks to be taken to an apartment, and when the people let her out, she disappears—seemingly into nothing. There is a wet spot on the car seat. People have checked residents of the apartment and no one knows anything about her. The girl always says that she was with a boy and that he had left her at the lake after trying to drown her. The legend is about three or four years old, and has been discussed in Dallas papers and on the radio.

> Mary E. Hill, Dallas

Grave

When you get chilled, a possum is walking over your grave.

> Mike Luna, Bay City
> Mrs. Smith, Bay City

Don't dip water out of a grave or you or someone dear to you will die.

> Jim Merrith, Lubbock
> Ed Cox, Lubbock

Hair

When someone in the family dies, if you comb your hair, change your clothes, clean house, or change anything, someone else in the family will die.

> Earlene Kay Ellis, Longview

Jump

If you jump over someone, you have to jump back over him or your mother will die.

> Hilda Ramirez, Beeville
> Eleanor H. Wilson, Beeville

Lamp

If a lamp goes out unexpectedly three times in a row, this is an indication that the master of the house has been killed in an accident.

> Edith Meade, Houston
> Jo Harris, Houston

Owl

All my life when an owl came to me and screeched or hooted, death or trouble of a serious nature came to me, or to my family soon afterwards.

> Ruby L. Mitchell, Houston
> Ray Wood, Raywood

When you hear an owl hoot, someone will die. You must say three times, "Go, evil spirit." Otherwise it will not go away.

> Mrs. R. S. Sutton, San Antonio
> Gordon Sutton, San Antonio

To stop a hooting owl at night that will bring death to the family, throw salt into the fire.

> Mrs. Emma Moody, Mansfield
> Susie M. Allen, Fort Worth

Pictures

When a person dies, any pictures you might have of him should be covered up.

> Stanley Marcus, Dallas

Pillow

When someone is dying, his feather pillow has a wreath or circle of feathers forming inside. If you open the pillow and break the circle, the person will recover.

> Joanne Howard, McKinney

Quail

If you eat a quail a day for thirty days, it will kill you.

> John Keener, Dallas
> Michael Keener, Dallas

DEATH AND BURIAL

Rats

When rats desert any vessel, it will not return from its next trip to sea.

> Gene Johnson, Dallas
> Larry Taylor, Dallas

Rooster

A rooster crowing after sundown or at midnight is a portent of death in the family.

> Paul Patterson, Crane

Saucer

If you bury a murdered man with a saucer on his chest, his killer will confess.

> June Vernon, Brownwood
> N. Yongue, Brownwood

Shoes

If you put your shoes higher than your head, it will cause a death.

> Mrs. Lemwell East, Austin
> Mrs. Maura Darrouzet, Austin

Silver Ring

Wearing a handmade silver ring will prevent death by snake bite and may prevent the snake bite itself.

> Jean Dugat, Beeville

Spider

If a spider has walked across a plate, it must be washed before being used, or the user will die.

> Donna Mobley, Austin
> Jim T. Mobley, Austin

Star

A falling star means a soul has gone to heaven.

V. M. Thompson, El Paso
Mary Ann Thompson, El Paso

Sundown

When you dig a grave, always have the corpse buried before sundown; never let the sun set on an open grave.

G. T. Summy, Whitesboro
H. D. Odom, Whitesboro

Sweet Potato

If you have a sweet potato vine in your house, someone will die.

Marcy Karen Russell, Houston
Mrs. John Russell, Houston

Toad

If a brown horned toad with a blue tongue bites you, it means certain death.

John Sanders, Austin

Whippoorwill

If you hear a whippoorwill near your house, it is a sign that one of the occupants will die.

Woodrow Kuhn, Austin
Larry Taylor, Dallas

Window

If you climb in through a window, you have to climb back out, or your mother will die.

Hilda Ramirez, Beeville
Eleanor H. Wilson, Beeville

Woodpecker

When a woodpecker pecks on your house daily for about three days or a week, there will be a death in the family.

Mrs. Sadie Young, Lufkin
Mrs. Bernice L. Harris, Lufkin

HUMAN BODY, FOLK MEDICINE

Arthritis

For pellagra, arthritis, cancer, tuberculosis, fill a pint jar with raisins and cover the raisins with straight whiskey. Let set for two weeks. Take two raisins a day like capsules.

Mrs. G. A. Rigby, Dayton
Frances Northcutt, Dayton

To ward off arthritis, wear a coppr band around your wrist. Either a copper wire or a copper bracelet will do.

Mrs. Selmon Moss, Aubrey
Peggy Callaway, Denton

Asthma

Cure for asthma attack: grind deer horns and make a tea.
Verna M. Thompson, Houston
George Fuermann, Houston

Asthma and tuberculosis can be cured with a syrup made by boiling silkweed root, adding honey and pine tar in equal quantities. The mixture is to be taken at least three times daily until the person is well.

Annie Mae Jackson, Pilot Point
Katherine C. Eberly, Denton

A mixture of wild plum bark, sugar, and whiskey boiled will stop asthma attack.

Mary Foreman, San Antonio
Sandra Freeman, Austin

If you have a child with asthma, the way to get rid of the asthma is to take the child to a sweet gum tree in the woods, back him up to it, and put a hole in the tree above his head. Take a twig of his hair and put it in the tree and make him walk away without looking back. When he grows taller than the mark on that tree, he will have lost his asthma.

>Mr. and Mrs. R. W. Fults, Center
>Jerry Fults, Center

To cure asthma, wind a copper wire around your neck and sleep all night with it on. The next morning the asthma will be gone.

>Ralph Eberly, Denton

Sleeping with a Mexican Chihuahua will cure asthma.

>Nancy Ann Hunt, Denton
>Marian Daniel, Denton

Athlete's Foot

Cow manure which is warm and fresh will kill athlete's foot fungus when applied just once.

>Howark Hanks, Denton

Baldness

Touching mushrooms on a rainy day causes baldness.

>Richard Martin, Carrollton
>Sarah Jackson, Carrollton

Bat

If a bat bites you on the neck, heat an iron red hot in the fire and touch it to the wound. Then put holy water on it.

>Juan Vega, Brownsville
>Pat DeViney, Austin

Bed Wetting

Sure cures for bed wetting are fried wharf rat or cow dung tea.

Carroll Rich, Denton

Brown some egg shells, crush them, put sugar on them, and eat them. This will stop bed wetting.

Walter Kramer, Kerrville
Mary Lehmann, Kerrville

Bites

Taking a hair from the dog that bit you will cure the bite.

Tim Webb, Houston
Mrs. Jo Harris, Houston

A madstone, a stone taken from an albino deer, when applied to any poisonous bite will draw out the poison. It will stick to the person's body as long as there is poison in the system.

Mrs. W. M. Baugh, Brownwood
Mrs. R. D. Belvin, Brownwood

Bleeding

Put a handful of soot on the bleeding spot and wrap tightly.

Mrs. Minnie Shaitzer, El Paso
Margaret Divelbiss, El Paso

To stop bleeding: put cobwebs on the wound. Soak the wound in kerosene. Bleeding can also be stopped by reading Ezekiel 16:6.

Mrs. T. C. Allen, Temple
Roy Lynn Boutwell, Temple

To stop the bleeding from a knife-inflicted wound, take the knife into the back yard and stick it into the ground.

Allan Jones, Fort Worth
Wynelle Ray, Fort Worth

Blemishes

If you wash in water that is standing in an oak stump, it will remove blemishes.

>Ronnie Fox, San Antonio
>John Igo, San Antonio

Blister

Pick a blister after sundown and it won't cause a sore.

>Mrs. Wiley Mosier, Dallas
>Shirley Dean Mosier, Dallas

Blood

Drink sassafras tea in the spring to thin the blood.

>Mrs. E. C. Hunt, El Paso
>Janet Irvin, El Paso

You will dry up your blood if you eat a lemon every day.

>Mrs. De La Cruz, Austin
>Barbara Ann Simota, Austin

Blood Pressure

Eat parsley for high blood pressure.

>Mrs. C. Spearman, El Paso
>Janet Irvin, El Paso

Eat garlic for high blood pressure.

>Mrs. E. C. Hunt, El Paso
>Janet Irvin, El Paso

Boils

For boils, make a poultice of bacon rind or of prickly pear.

>Mrs. Agnes Cocke, Austin
>Jim Davis, Austin

To cure boils, catch a wild roadrunner, broil him and eat him.

> James M. Somach, Del Rio
> James M. Spray, Dallas

For a boil, use white foam from stem of a fig tree, rubbed on the boil.

> Mr. De La Cruz, Austin
> Barbara Ann Simota, Austin

For boils or stone bruises, use scrapings of homemade lye soap mixed with a tablespoon or two of sugar molasses and applied as a salve or poultice.

> Chester V. Kielman, Austin
> David B. Gracy, Austin

Put cow manure poultice on boils and stone bruises.

> Judy Harbour, Austin
> Judy Hicks, Austin

Chopped onions cure boils.

> Mrs. Perry Mayes, Rock Springs
> Mrs. Regina Koeniger, Fort Worth

Boils may be brought to a head by applying a wilted cabbage leaf.

> Mrs. Robert Tayes, New Braunfels
> Sondra Pittman, Corpus Christi

Burns

This is for major burns. Rub butter on the burn for five to ten minutes. Then brown ½ cup of flour and put it in cheesecloth. Dust this on wound—it will help bring the color back.

> R. S. Masterson, Austin

The pain will soon leave if you make a paste of ground raw potato and hold it on a burn.

> Georgia Castro, Austin
> Anne Hartley Sutherland, Austin

Apply soda and molasses or linseed oil.

> Mrs. Agnes Cocke, Austin
> Jim Davis, Austin

Soda and vanilla extract paste is good to relieve the pain of burns.

> Mrs. Brown, Austin
> Judy Hicks, Austin

Cactus

"When my sister was sick, my mother got a big cactus and measured my sister's foot—put the foot on the cactus and drew around it and cut it out. Then she hung it outside, and when it was dry my sister was okay."

> Pete Ybarra, Brownsville
> Pat DeViney, Austin

Cancer

Cooking foods in aluminum utensils will cause cancer of the stomach.

> Mrs. Cannon, Austin
> Barbara Ann Simota, Austin

Chicken Pox

If a child has chicken pox, send him into a chicken coop and shoo the chickens over his head. This should immediately cure him.

> Ruth Green, San Antonio
> Sandra Freeman, Austin

If you have the chicken pox, tear a jet black chicken open and rub the blood on the sores, and they will go away.

> Mr. and Mrs. R. W. Fults, Center
> Jerry Fults, Center

Coffee

If a person drinks coffee at a young age he will get black behind his ears.

> Charles Manuel Flores, San Antonio
> Irene Seidensticker, San Antonio

Colds

Red onions boiled with sugar are given to children for colds.

> Mary Foreman, San Antonio
> Sandra Freeman, Austin

Boil potatoes and leave them in their skins. After this, put them on and around your feet. This is supposed to cure a cold.

> Ofelia Ramirez, El Paso
> Ann Foster, El Paso

Save old bread until it gets mildew on it. Eat it to cure colds.

> Mabel Oliver, Houston
> Coy Howard, Austin

For cold, cough, or sore throat: take mullen tea, or turpentine and sugar, or horehound tea, or honey and whiskey, or hot lemonade.

> Mrs. Agnes Cocke, Austin
> Jim Davis, Austin

To cure a baby's cold, hang an ace and two queens at the head of his bed to take away the spirits that cause the cold.

> Mike Killinger, Brownsville
> Pat DeViney, Austin

Yerba de la víbora is good for colds. Boil this weed with two drops of turpentine. Drink the mixture while it is still hot.

> Mrs. Esperanza Burns, El Paso
> Margaret Divelbiss, El Paso

For a bad cold or sore throat, eat *jalapeño* peppers or chili that is very hot.

> Alma P. Miller, El Paso

If you have a cold, tie a red ant on a string around your neck.

> Barbara Hurt, El Paso
> Janet Irvin, El Paso

To prevent colds, paint the bottoms of your feet with iodine.

> L. L. Jones, Fort Worth
> Wynelle Ray, Fort Worth

Rub onion and skunk oil on the chest for a chest cold.

> Mrs. Cotton Ross, Austin
> Judy Hicks, Austin

Before going out in the cool of the evening in a low-necked dress, a girl should put some cold water on her chest to avoid catching cold.

> Mrs. W. D. Young, San Antonio
> Barbara South, San Antonio

Boil button willow roots with wild cherry bark. Then mix this tea with good whiskey and rock candy made from ribbon cane syrup.

> Mrs. Ruby Knight, Mineola
> Dallas S. Lankford, IV, Mineola

Consumption

Consumption may be cured by drinking hot bat's blood, or by swallowing a rattlesnake heart live, or by smearing the chest with grease from a black cat.

> Mrs. W. D. Young, San Antonio
> Barbara South, San Antonio

Corns

Use rattlesnake oil to cure corns, calluses, bunions, and hard skin on the heels.

> Mrs. De La Cruz, Austin
> Barbara Ann Simota, Austin

Cough

No cure for a cough is as good as smoking a pipeful of dry cowchip. This will also keep the mosquitoes away.

> William D. Wittliff, Austin

Cramps

To get rid of leg cramps, place your shoe soles up under your bed when you go to sleep at night.

> Mrs. Charles A. Mitchell, Granado
> Jean Dugat, Beeville

Crick

To get rid of a crick in your neck, go where a hog has rubbed his body on a tree and left some of the mud on the tree. You should then rub your neck just as he does.

> Mandy Spencer, Houston
> George Fuermann, Houston

Crying

When cutting or peeling onions, hold a match in your mouth and you won't cry.

> Mrs. Eugene Butler, Dallas

Cut

If you cut your leg or foot on a barbed wire fence, rub lard on the barb to prevent infection.

> Johnny Johnson, Lubbock
> Ed Cox, Lubbock

If you have a cut, you should chew up a piece of homemade bread with butter on it. Place it on the cut, and it will heal.

> Mrs. Hugo Kopplin, Three Rivers
> Dora Kopplin, Beeville

Cyst

Strike a cyst with a Bible to make it go away.

> Lucy Mae Johnson, Tyler
> Mary Darrah, Fort Worth

Diarrhea

Peel bark back on hickory tree and chew greenish bark filled with the sap of the tree.

> Verna M. Thompson, Houston
> George Fuermann, Houston

Earache

Scorch a granddaddy-longlegs spider in a coal-oil lamp. Wrap it in cotton after removing the legs. Then insert it in the afflicted ear.

> Mrs. Carter, Manchaca
> Ramsey Wiggins and Ann Arnold, Austin

Tie a string to a pod of garlic, place the garlic pod in the ear and wear for three days.

> Charles Holik, Caldwell
> Margaret Hooper, Temple

Boil a mixture of onions and tobacco in water. Drop the juice from the mixture into the ear.

> Mrs. Alta Johnson, Dayton
> Frances Northcutt, Dayton

Blow smoke into the ear and hold hand over the ear for a few minutes.

> Mrs. John Ogdon, Austin
> Jim Davis, Austin

Kill a rattlesnake and boil in a washpot. Skim oil from the top and drop warm into the ear. The oil can be kept in a bottle for future use.

> Andrew Jackson Brown, Flatonia
> Wilson M. Hudson, Austin

Make a small cloth sack and partially fill with salt. Warm the sack on the stove and place on the ear. The salt will hold the heat.

> Ann Byrd Brown, Flatonia
> Wilson M. Hudson, Austin

Epilepsy

To cure a child of epileptic fits, the child's father must have his wife take his little finger, cut it, and squeeze three drops of blood into a spoon and give the blood to the child.

> Mrs. T. C. Allen, Temple
> Roy Lynn Boutwell, Temple

Eye

If you are worried about something and want to get it off your mind, light a match and watch it burn out—the first half with your right eye only and the other half with your left eye.

> Gilbert Valdez, San Antonio
> Irene Seidensticker, San Antonio

This is a quick cure for sore eyes. Get some watermelon vines and leaves and boil them a few minutes. Then thicken with cornmeal or wheat bran. Put the mixture in a thin white cloth. When it gets cool, apply another batch to the eyes in the same cloth.

> Rickey Mercer, Gainesville
> Don Pope, Gainesville

To remove particles in the eye, boil an egg for one minute. Place the white of the egg on a clean white cloth and apply to eye.

> Mrs. Lewis Forke, New Braunfels
> Sondra Pittman, Corpus Christi

Carrots will uncross a baby's eyes if they are fed to him while he is still young.

> Mrs. J. H. Cone, El Paso
> Ann Foster, El Paso

Face

Never make a face. The clock may strike when you are making it. If it does, your face will stay that way always.

> Mrs. E. E. Gilbert, Camp Wood
> Lana Gildart, Camp Wood

Feet

To cure stinking feet, take sea sand and put it in a bucket large enough to put your feet in. If it has lost its moisture, put enough water in to moisten it thoroughly. Place your feet in it and keep them there for two hours every day until the stink leaves. It usually takes three or four days to have "stinkless feet."

> Ray Overstreet, San Antonio
> Jean Dugat, Beeville

If you sleep with your feet out from under the covers, a wolf will bite your toe.

>Mrs. Emma Moore, Dallas
>Jeanne Caldwell, Russell, Kansas

Fertility

Drinking a mixture of honey and vinegar before going to bed each night will help make you fertile.

>Jack Walters, Houston
>Coy Howard, Austin

Fever

Tea from boiled goat pills, tied up in a nice clean rag, cures fever.

>Mrs. Perry Mayes, Rock Springs
>Mrs. Regina Koeniger, Fort Worth

To get rid of a fever, apply a poultice of mashed onions to stomach, armpits, soles of the feet, and palms of the hands.

>Mrs. Alta Johnson, Dayton
>Frances Northcutt, Dayton

Wear lily leaves tied around the head to ward off fever.

>Mrs. Alta Johnson, Dayton
>Frances Northcutt, Dayton

To get rid of chills and fever, boil one part cottonseed in two parts water. Strain and drink.

>Mrs. Alta Johnson, Dayton
>Frances Northcutt, Dayton

To get rid of fever, clip a nail of the patient; put it in a bag with an eel. When the eel dies, the fever will leave.

>Geral T. Allen, Dallas

Take ground frogs' heads for fever.

Geral T. Allen, Dallas

Wind spider webs from the north side of a barn and take.

Geral T. Allen, Dallas

Pound a snake's body until it's dead. Soak it in white wine and add opium. Take the liquid drawn off.

Geral T. Allen, Dallas

Fever Blisters

Ear wax is good to apply to fever blisters. It's not a cure, but the taste of the wax is so bitter that you won't want to lick your lips.

Bessie Toney, El Paso
John Jimerson, El Paso

Fingernail

Collect your fingernail and toenail clippings, because anyone who gets possession of them can use them to put a hex on you.

Howard Hanks, Denton

The number of white marks on your fingernails reveals the number of lies you have told. A variation concerning this is that the marks reveal the number of boyfriends or girlfriends you have.

Susan Hayes Long, Denton

Fits

Fits can be instantly cured by throwing a spoonful of fine salt as far back into the mouth of the patient as possible, just as the fit comes on.

Mrs. W. E. Gunn, Freeport
Coy Howard, Austin

Freckles

If you want to remove freckles from your skin, bathe them with stagnant water taken from an old tree stump.

> G. Liles, Pasadena
> Larry Taylor, Dallas

If you wash your face with buttermilk before 6:00 a.m., your freckles will go away.

> Mary Ann Michum, Waco
> Lella C. Ward, Waco

To get rid of freckles, put buttermilk on your face and let a cat lick it off.

> Mandy Spencer, Houston
> George Fuermann, Houston

Collect dew from the grass at midnight on May 1 and rub it on your face. Your freckles will go away.

> Mrs. J. V. Kvacek, Fort Worth
> Shirley Horner, Fort Worth

Gargle

A good mix for a gargle is ground grasshoppers and coal oil.

> Geral T. Allen, Dallas

Hair

If the birds get your hair after you've gotten a haircut and build a nest with it, it will drive you crazy.

> Bessie Toney, El Paso
> John Jimerson, El Paso

The black part of chicken feces rubbed on an adolescent boys' chest will cause hair to grow and make him look manly.

> Sid Cox, College Station

Hangover

Boil *el huevo de torro,* a weed, and drink it for a hangover.

Mrs. Esperanza Burns, El Paso
Margaret Divelbiss, El Paso

Harm

If you feel that some kind of harm is going to happen to you, sprinkle your shoe with red pepper to ward off all evil.

Mrs. Lucille Carlisle, El Paso
John Jimerson, El Paso

Hay Fever

Take a few doses of rhubarb and a dose of quinine at night for hay fever.

Mrs. Polly Green, Dayton
Frances Northcott, Dayton

Honeycomb chewed every day for one month before hay fever season begins will prevent an attack or make it milder.

Dr. Arthur Mores, Lufkin
Mary Alice Darrah, Fort Worth

Head

Sleeping with your head lower than your feet will increase your intelligence.

Patricia Jetton, Denton

Headache

Burning human hair gives the former owner a headache.

Jean George, Port Neches

If you walk directly in the footsteps of another person, you will have a headache for three days.

Dwain Anderson, Palestine

If you walk in another's tracks, it will give him a headache.

>Shirley Covington, Center
>Mrs. Vivian Hyer, Center

If you walk on your enemy's grave, you will have a headache.

>Mrs. Ollie B. Wilson, Plainview
>James W. Wilson, Sanger

To cure a headache, pull the thorns from a cactus pad. Then peel the cactus and lay it across the forehead to let the juice of the cactus flow freely over the forehead.

>Diane Haigler, San Antonio
>John Igo, San Antonio

Health, General

To keep healthy, use this stimulating liniment: 2 pounds hog lard, 1 pound rosin, ½ pound beeswax, ¼ pound cayenne pepper, well melted together over a fire. Take it from the fire and stir it until you can bear your finger in it, then add 1 ounce sassafras oil. Stir well together until nearly cold.

>Hardeman Family Papers, 1848–1869
>David B. Gracy, Austin

Heart

For heart trouble, boil a roadrunner (paisano) and eat it.

>Ulunda Garcia, Austin
>Barbara Ann Simota, Austin

Hiccoughs

Pull your tongue out as far as possible and hold until the count of ten.

>Mrs. John Ogdon, Austin
>Jim Davis, Austin

Take off your shoes, and after wetting your right forefinger with saliva, cross the toe of your left shoe three times while reciting the Lord's Prayer three times rapidly in succession.

> Alene Greene, San Antonio
> Barbara South, San Antonio

Put your head in a plastic bag and breathe in and out for five minutes. Take your head out, blow up the bag, and burst it. Your hiccoughs will be cured for good.

> Larry Smith, Hamilton

Hives

To prevent a baby from having hives, take the white part of fresh chicken excrement, boil in tea, and give to the baby.

> Mrs. E. B. Frazar, Austin
> Jim Davis, Austin

To cure hives, apply parched honeybees to the area.

> Mrs. Josie Bost, Novice
> Roy W. Bost, Dallas

Illness, Prevention of

A person who sees a caterpillar should spit in order to prevent illness.

> Kathryn White, Pasadena
> Larry Taylor, Dallas

Itch

To cure the itch, boil pokeberry roots and bathe the itch in the water.

> H. D. Odom, Whitesboro

Kidney

A tea made from watermelon or pumpkin seeds is good for kidney ailments.

> Mrs. Robert Tayes, New Braunfels
> Sondra Pittman, Corpus Christi

Limb

To make your limbs supple and limber, cook a buzzard down to grease and grease your limbs with it.

> Mrs. Sadie Young, Lufkin
> Mrs. Bernice L. Harris, Lufkin

Malaria

For treatment of malaria, drink a cup of fresh cow urine.

> Mrs. E. B. Frazar, Austin
> Jim Davis, Austin

For malaria, suck on pieces of iron.

> Mrs. E. B. Frazar, Austin
> Jim Davis, Austin

Measles

Cow-chip (manure) tea is good for measles.

> Ruth Green, San Antonio
> Sandra Freeman, Austin

Menstruation

Hair will not take a permanent curl during menstruation.

> Mrs. De La Cruz, Austin
> Barbara Ann Simota, Austin

Mumps

To heal the mumps, rub fish oil behind each ear and over the throat. Then cover with a cloth.

> Ruth Green, San Antonio
> Sandra Freeman, Austin

For mumps, wrap your throat in fig leaves or cottonwood leaves.

> Mrs. Esperanza Burns, El Paso
> Margaret Divelbiss, El Paso

Smear mumps with tar off of a buggy wheel.

> Mrs. Esperanza Burns, El Paso
> Margaret Divelbiss, El Paso

Mustache, Color of

Beware of that man, be he friend or brother,
Whose hair is one color, and mustache another.

> Mrs. Tonie Lesovsky, Cameron
> Margaret Gresham, Temple

Nosebleed

To stop nosebleed, tear a small scrap from a paper bag and put it between the gums and teeth in the upper part of the mouth.

> Mrs. Polly Green, Dayton
> Frances Northcutt, Dayton

To stop nosebleed, hang a door key down the back of your neck, or chew a piece of paper that has been written on on the opposite side.

> Mrs. P. B. Blayney, Irving
> Dennis Redfearn, Dallas

Pneumonia

Take the patient out to the barn, cover him with a blanket, then cover him with fresh manure.

> Mrs. E. B. Frazar, Austin
> Jim Davis, Austin

Pregnancy

Tie a thread to a pregnant woman's wedding ring and dangle it over her stomach. If the ring swings back and forth, the baby will be a boy; if the ring twirls around, she will have a girl.

> William D. Wittliff, Austin

Rheumatism

Sleep with a Mexican hairless dog.

> Mrs. G. A. Rigby, Dayton
> Frances Northcutt, Dayton

Ringworm

Rub a copper penny moistened with saliva on the ringworm.

> Alene Greene, San Antonio
> Barbara South, San Antonio

The juice from the hulls of green black walnuts is good for ringworms.

> Mary Foreman, San Antonio
> Sandra Freeman, Austin

To cure ringworm, rub the milk from a fig leaf on it.

> Mabel Oliver, Houston
> Coy Howard, Austin

Sick

"When my sister was sick, we wrapped her in a sheet and laid her in the dirt. Then we took a knife and drew around her body. My mother took an egg and made the sign of the cross on my sister's body while she was saying prayers. Then she but the broken egg in water near my sister for twenty-four hours."

        Juan Vega, Brownsville
        Pat DeViney, Austin

Side Pain

To cure a pain in the side, spit on a rock and throw it over the left shoulder.

        Mrs. Pat Sheridan, Matador

When you are running and you get a bad pain in your side from running too long, if you will lean over and spit under a small rock from the side opposite the pain, it will quit.

        Jerry Fults, Center
        Mrs. Vivian Hyer, Center

Sleep

Don't sleep with your head toward the fire; it will bake your brain and make you crazy.

        Alan Dale Brown, San Saba
        Carroll Rich, Denton

Smallpox

Use watermelon juice for smallpox.

        Mrs. Esperanza Burns, El Pazo
        Margaret Divelbliss, El Paso

Sore

A sore can be cured by letting a dog lick it.

        Mrs. W. D. Young, San Antonio
        Barbara South, San Antonio

Spasms

Scrape grease from around a man's hatband and make a tea to give to babies with spasms.

R. S. Masterson, Austin

Splinter

Draw out a splinter by sugar and soap poultice. Scrape soap shavings into your hand. Work in a teaspoon of sugar, then moisten with water. Apply to bandage of cloth and tape on the wound. Overnight the splinter will be drawn to the surface.

Verna M. Thompson, Houston
George Fuermann, Houston

Sprained Ankle

For a sprained ankle, moisten red clay with vinegar to make a poultice to pack around the ankle. Then wrap the ankle in brown paper.

Verna M. Thompson, Houston
George Fuermann, Houston

Stomach-ache

A stomach-ache can be cured by hanging a pair of trousers upside down.

Mrs. Pat Sheridan, Matador

Sty

To get rid of a sty, repeat the following rhyme:
   Go to the crossroads, leave my eye,
   Catch the first fool that passes by.

Mrs. John Ogden, Austin
Jim Davis, Austin

Rub the end of a cat's tail on a sty to cure the sty.

Mable Oliver, Houston
Coy Howard, Austin

Teeth

When your wisdom teeth come in, half of your life is supposed to be over.

                        Charlene Allison, Dallas
                        Gerald B. Pratt, Dallas

Nine live red ants worn in a bag around the neck will help the baby in teething.

                        Olive Jane Strange, Temple
                        Margaret Gresham, Temple

To keep the baby from having teething pains, rub his gums with the brains of a rabbit.

                        Mrs. Pat Sheridan, Matador

To keep the baby from having trouble while teething, the mother should bite the head from a live mouse.

                        Mrs. Pat Sheridan, Matador

Thrash (Thrush)

For the thrash, sores in a child's mouth, tie a bag of thirteen sow bugs around the child's neck. When the bugs die, the child will be well.

                        Mrs. Mollie Fry, Brownwood
                        Mrs. R. D. Belvin, Brownwood

Throat

If a bone is caught in your throat, eat a piece of cornbread and swallow lots of water.

                        Ruth Green, San Antonio
                        Sandra Freeman, Austin

For a sore throat, take a tomato and rub it on your feet and then on your throat.

                        Juan Vega, Brownsville
                        Pat DeViney, Austin

Tonsils

If your tonsils are sore, take the saliva from someone who is well. Rub it on the outside of your neck, and it will cure them.

    Mr. Diaz, Austin
    Barbara Ann Simota, Austin

Toothache

Biting on a nail will stop a toothache.

    Mr. and Mrs. Frazer, Austin
    Jim Davis, Austin

Tooth Decay

Wearing a rattlesnake rattler in the back of a hat will prevent tooth decay.

    Myrna Whitman, Port Neches

Tuberculosis

To cure tuberculosis, take a live jet black dog, throw him into a pot of boiling water and cook him down to a soup. Allow the person a teaspoonful three times a day.

    Mrs. Sadie Young, Lufkin
    Mrs. Bernice L. Harris, Lufkin

Typhoid

To cure typhoid, cut an onion in quarters and place one quarter in each corner of the room.

    Burle M. Martin, Dallas
    Roger Middleton, Dallas

Ulcer

Take alum and you won't have an ulcer.

    Janice Yates, Denton
    Jo Ann Boyd, Denton

Urinating

If you urinate in the street, a bump will come on your eye.

> Charles Hunter, Denton
> Mrs. G. Adams, Denton

Warts

The following is the informant's account of a "cure" which her Negro maid, Maudie Reese, performed on Mardi when she lived in Tupelo, Mississippi:

"When I was about four years old I had quite a few warts on my hands, knees, and elbows. Maudie wanted to conjure them off, but Mama wouldn't let her. So one week-end when my parents went out of town, Maudie conjured off my warts by sticking a gold pin in a wart, putting the blood in the chickens' drinking water. Then she walked away without looking back, leaving my warts in the chickens' water. It worked, too. I've never had any warts since."

> Mardi Young, Austin
> Barbara South, San Antonio

To make warts go away, sit in a cemetery for three nights in a row. Next, find a fresh grave and lay flowers on it, wishing the warts away. Two weeks later the warts will fall off.

> Vic Ratton, Baytown
> Mary Darrah, Fort Worth

If you have warts, set a rusty can out before sunrise and catch the morning rain. Then boil an egg in this water. Next, make three holes in the egg, leaving the shell on. Take the egg and put it in the middle af an ant bed. When the ants have completely eaten the inside of the egg, your warts will be gone.

> Mrs. Maxey, Lubbock
> Kay Clapp, Lubbock

Put horse manure on a wart to remove it.

> Ruth Green, San Antonio
> Sandra Freeman, Austin

Worms

The bark of the avocado tree or its seed covering when boiled in water is a good medicine for children who have internal worms.

>Jimmy Martinez, Austin
>Barbara Ann Simota, Austin

Wounds

Chicken manure will heal deep wounds.

>Dr. Nina Harris, College Station
>Mrs. John Q. Anderson, College Station

NUMBERS, SEASONS, TIMES OF DAY

August

If you want posts to stay in the ground solidly, put them in in August.

>Pleas Vaughan, Sanger
>James M. Wilson, Sanger

Corn

It is corn planting time when the leaves on the oak trees are as big as a squirrel's ear.

>J. F. Lasiter, Whitesboro
>H. D. Odum, Whitesboro

Eleven

Always count backward from eleven to one whenever you forget something and have to go back after it.

>Kathy Conlon, Midlothian

February

If the wind blows from the north on the fourteenth of February, there will be a good fruit crop.

>Mrs. J. W. Ford, Corsicana
>Jean Dugat, Beeville

Friday

It is bad luck to take ashes out on Friday.

>Mrs. Ray Hamilton, Rising Star
>N. Young, Brownwood

Never cut any kind of garment on a Friday. If you do, the garment will never be completed.

>Mrs. C. W. Ralston, Midlothian
>Judy Ralston, Midlothian

Eve tempted Adam with the fatal apple on Friday. The flood in the Bible, the confusion in the tower of Babel, and the death of Jesus Christ all took place on Friday.

>Jerry Fults, Center
>Mrs. Vivian Hyer, Center

Good Friday

A person who digs in the earth on Good Friday will see blood.

>Mrs. Josephine Watson, Groves
>James Lee McCutcheon, Groves

July 30

If you open a can of paint on July 30, you will go crazy.

>Keith Copeland, Brownsville
>Pat DeViney, Austin

May Day

If it rains on the first day of May (May Day), it will rain half of the days in May.

>George W. McElhany, Athens
>Mrs. Eva Coleman, Denton

New Year's Day

Eat stuffed cabbage and green peas on New Year's Day for good luck the rest of the year.

Maude Romero, Robstown
Jan Crain, Austin

Don't sweep dirt over the threshold on New Year's Day, because it will cause a bad year.

Cora Jan Fitzgerald, Knox City
Mrs. Ottis Cash, Knox City

Night

Chewing gum at night is actually chewing a dead man's bones.

Anita J. Zuniga, Mercedes
T. M. Harwell, Edinburg

St. John's Day

If a girl cuts off a little hair on St. John's Day, it will grow four times as long by the next anniversary.

Barbara Ann Simota, Austin

Saturday

Don't get married on Saturday. Your marriage won't last.

Robin Smith, Lubbock
Mrs. Ralph T. Caldwell, Lubbock

Seventh

My great-grandmother is the seventh daughter of a seventh daughter, and she seems to have magical power of some kind. She refuses to use her power unless in an emergency, because she insists that it is wichcraft. She can rub her gold wedding ring to remove a wart or sty. She cured my aunt from the thrash (thrush) when she was a small baby by taking her into a closed room and blowing into the baby's mouth.

Anne Arnold, Seagoville
Linda Elsey, Seagoville

Sunday

There is no harm in sewing on Sunday, if you do not use a thimble.

Ray Wood, Raywood

Embarrassment is believed to be caused by clipping the toenails or by expulsion of body gases on Sunday.

Mrs. G. M. Trejo, Austin
Ricardo Everett, Austin

Three

If the snow stays on the ground three days in succession, it will snow again.

Harold Levine, Gainesville
Charles R. Horn, Gainesville

If you lose your dog, whistle three times through a knothole and he will return.

Mrs. Ruby Mann, Houston
Ray Wood, Raywood

Winter

Put cow's milk in a fruit jar nearly full of water and watch it. If it clears up fast, you can expect a mild winter. But if it stays cloudy and foggy for a long time, there is going to be a bad, cold, wet winter.

Ophelia Thompson, Whitesboro
H. D. Odom, Whitesboro

Yard

Those who talk by the yard and think by the inch should be removed by the foot.

R. L. Gatewood, Dallas
Jimmy Wells, Dallas

TRADES AND PROFESSIONS

Crops

If you cut some hair from the head of a dead person and plant it with your seed, you will have good crops.

>Richard Hinojosa, Brownsville
>Pat DeViney, Austin

Sleep only east and west or your crops won't grow.

>Robert F. Moon, Denton

Farmers

Redheaded farmers raise more carrots than anyone else, and the best red peppers.

>W. F. Harper, Denton
>Jim Edwards, Denton

Financial Loss

If you count your profits too much, you will have great financial loss.

>J. L. Taylor, Dallas
>Larry Taylor, Dallas

Lineman

If a lineman should fall from a utility pole, he must climb it again immediately, or he will never climb again, or else he will always be afraid.

>Joe Barker, Childress
>L. H. Tucker, Denton

Manufacturer

In the retailing business, if a manufacturer drops a dress on the floor by accident, this means that it will be a good seller.

>Stanley Marcus, Dallas

It's customary for a soloist performer (musician) to give his accompanist a penny for luck immediately before a concert. The receiver carries the gift on stage with him.

> Richard H. Wood, Freeport
> Marian Daniel, Denton

SPORTS

Baseball

If a pitcher strikes out the first batter he faces in a baseball game, he will lose the game.

> Jerry Campbell, Center

If you are a baseball announcer, never mention that a pitcher is pitching a no-hitter, or he will lose the game.

> Johnny Lewis, Denton

It is good luck to wear one black and one white shoelace when playing baseball.

> Skip White, Austin
> Bob Watts, Austin

It is good luck to wear a longer stocking on your left leg than on your right leg while playing baseball.

> Butch Thompson, Austin
> Bob Watts, Austin

Baseball players should not wash their suits if they have a winning streak going.

> Marian Daniel, Denton

Many major leaguers are cautious of lending their bats to other players, for they believe that there are a certain number of hits in each bat, and they don't want the other player to have one of their hits.

> Marion Thompson, Angleton
> Grace Wellborn, Lubbock

Bowler

When a bowler has a string of strikes, it is considered bad luck to add up his score until the string is complete, or the string will be broken.

> Joan Kay Trabucco, San Antonio
> John Igo, San Antonio

Boxing

Before a boxing match, never eat rabbit meat, because you will be timid like a rabbit.

> Marsha Williams, Lubbock
> Ed Cox, Lubbock

Bridge

Any Wacoan playing bridge who wanted to win would have to sit with his back to the Brazos.

> Mrs. H. R. Edwards, Waco

If the ace, two, three, and four are played in the same trick, all players may place their right hands on the cards, and their wishes will come true.

> Dorothy Tottenham, Denton

Clothes

If a coach has a winning streak, he wears the same clothes at every game or his luck will change.

> Mary K. Lewis, Denton
> Johnny Lewis, Denton

Dominos

For good luck when playing dominoes, put a handkerchief on your head and walk around the chair.

> Mrs. Bertha Reed, Lott
> Jean Dugat, Beeville

Fishing

If the cows are grazing, the fish are biting. When cows stop grazing, the fish stop biting.

"Eke" Daniel, McKinney
Bobbye Jack Minshew, McKinney

Wind from the south, fish bite with their mouth,
Wind from the east, fish bite least,
Wind from the north, don't go forth,
Wind from the west, fish bite best.

Mrs. Frank S. McKee, Fort Worth
Margaret Curl, Fort Worth

If you count the number of fish you have caught, you will catch no more that day.

Michael Wayne Cleveland, Longview

Fish bite best as the moon grows full.

Ramon Teal, Cameron
Marcus Teal, San Benito

The fishing is good when the bluebonnets are in bloom.

Frances L. Herring, San Antonio

Football

Some football teams touch goal line flags upon entering the field gor good luck.

Mary H. Zehr, San Antonio

Golf

Whenever a golf player putts into the hole, he immediately removes his ball, because it is believed that as long as the ball is in the hole, it jinxes the other balls, and keeps the other players from sinking their putts.

Eugene Mitchell, Austin
Bob Watts, Austin

SPORTS

Hunting

When you are out hunting, if you see a rabbit run up hill, you will have good luck.

> Kay Lynne Busbee, Comfort
> Neil Hawkins, Denton

Poker

It's bad luck to have both a pair of aces and a pair of eights in a poker game.

> Benny Lemanski, Denton
> Fleur Fuller, Denton

Racing

Among American racing drivers, green-painted cars are thought to bring bad luck.

> Joel Sappenfield, Denton
> Richard Earnhart, Denton

Rodeo

New boots will bring a cowboy good luck in a rodeo.

> Herman Sullivan, Carrizo Springs

When a rider in a rodeo goes into the arena, he must hold his rope first on the right side of the horse, then on the left on the second entrance, aternating again for every ride, to prevent bad luck.

> Ed Lohman, Monahans
> Marian Daniel, Denton

Tennis

In playing tennis, when you serve the first ball and it hits the net and bounces back to you, don't pick it up or you'll have bad luck.

> Nancy Deason, Beaumont
> Mary McCoy, Denton

Volleyball

Before every volleyball game strike your finger over your tongue and then strike a mirror. This is called licking the mirror.

> Ann Roberts, Crane
> Paul Patterson, Crane

WEATHER

Ants

When you are pestered with sugar ants, it is a sign that there is going to be a severe winter.

> Mrs. Sadie Young, Lufkin
> Mrs. Bernice L. Harris, Lufkin

If ants build high walls around their beds, it will rain.

> Mrs. Perry Mayes, Rock Springs
> Mrs. Regina Koeniger, Fort Worth

If the ants remain in their holes in the ground all day, a rainstorm is coming.

> Suzanne Hoyt, San Angelo
> James Davidson, Denton

Ax

If a bad cloud comes up and you want to get rid of it, take an ax, twirl it around your head three times, and throw it toward the cloud.

> Lovie Jane Green, Eldorado
> Charlie Henry, Groves

Bees

When bees stay close to the hive, rain is close by.

> Thomas C. Ward, Marlin
> Margaret Gresham, Temple

Cactus

When a cactus excretes juice around the stickers, it will soon rain.

R. E. Bigham, College Station

Cat

When you see the cat sitting on the hearth licking his paws, it is a sure sign of rain.

N. G. Curry, Big Sandy
Mrs. Johnnie I. Bendy, Mineola

Corn

If the shucks on ear corn are thick, it will be a long cold winter.

Harry D. Kilgore, Sherman

Cow

A cow coming from the pasture with her tail over her back is a sign that it will rain tomorrow.

Tania Morgan, Dallas

Cricket

Count the number of chirps a cricket makes in fifteen seconds, add forty, and you have the temperature.

R. E. Bigham, College Station

Crow

Crow on the fence, rain will go hence;
Crow on the ground, rain will come down.

Jerry Fults, Center
Mrs. Vivian Hyer, Center

Day

Evening red and morning gray,
Two sure signs of one fine day.

        Mrs. John R. Eidson, Hamilton

Fork

Stick a fork in the ground when it's raining, and it will stop.

        Linda Rai Heath, Athens
        A. C. Norman, Athens

Frog

Placing a dead frog on top of a post, feet upward, will cause rain.

        Ruby Trahan, Port Neches

Hail

When you want it to stop hailing, go outside and catch three hailstones in a dishpan.

        Larry Malone, Lubbock

Hog

If a hog is seen carrying sticks in its mouth, it is a sure sign of a blue norther.

        Wayne Lindley, Samnorwood
        Don Vanpelt, Samnorwood

Lightning

To keep lightning from striking your house during a storm, sit on a feather pillow.

        John Sanders, Austin

Moon

When the moon is on its back, it is a wet moon. When the moon is upside down, it is a dry moon, because the water has been poured out.

> Kyle McCain, Gainesville
> Charles R. Horn, Gainesville

If you can hang a bucket on the moon and not have it tilted, there will be dry weather.

> Mary Yarbrough, Center
> Mrs. Vivian Hyer, Center

Morning

Morning red and evening gray, sends the traveler on his way.
Morning gray and evening red, brings rain down upon his head.

> Price Woolridge, Lubbock
> Mrs. Ralph T. Caldwell, Lubbock

Norther

If more than thirteen blackbirds land on a fence, it is a sign of a norther.

> Carolyn Pekar, Port Lavaca
> Mrs. T. A. Carmichael, Port Lavaca

Okra

When the okra pod sheds its seeds, do not burn the pod, or it will cause a drouth.

> Tan Turner, Bowie

Onion

Onion's skin very thin, mild winter coming in;
Onion's skin thick and tough, coming winter cold and rough.

> Jerry Fults, Center
> Mrs. Vivian Hyer, Center

Rabbit

If the animals such as rabbits, armadillos, coons, and skunks move around a lot at night, there will be a change in the weather.

> Kay Lynne Busbee, Comfort
> Neil Hawkins, Denton

Rain

When killdeers holler on the hills, it will rain, or there will be a norther within three days.

> Mrs. Eugene Mayes, Rock Springs
> Mrs. Regina Koeniger, Fort Worth

If a whirlwind comes out of the southeast, there will be rain within twenty-four hours.

> Patricia Di Cuffa, Lubbock

If you break an "umbrella plant," it will rain.

> John Schrecengost, Denton
> Bob Cherry, Denton

Scorpions

If stinging scorpions crawl with their tails curled over their backs, it will rain.

> Mrs. Perry Mayes, Rock Springs
> Mrs. Regina Koeniger, Fort Worth

Sharks

When sharks jump out of the water, bad weather is brewing.

> J. A. Roberts, McAllen
> T. M. Harwell, Edinburg

Telephone Wires

When telephone wires hum and whine, a weather change is near.

        Mrs. Mildred McCracken, Temple
        Margaret Gresham, Temple

Terrapins

When tarantulas and terrapins cross the highway, it will rain.

        Bob Fry, Shannon
        Preston G. DeShazo, Dallas

Thunder

If it thunders while you are churning, the milk will sour.

        Mrs. A. F. Shepperd, Gladewater
        John Ben Shepperd, Odessa

Thunderstorm

Playing a piano during a thunderstorm will draw the lightning. Playing any musical instrument or singing will draw lightning.

        Mrs. F. O. Garnett, Jacksboro
        Sam George, Jr., Antelope

Be careful when taking a bath during a thunderstorm, because the water will draw lightning.

        Mrs. Felix R. McCoy, Fort Worth
        Mary F. McCoy, Fort Worth

Whistle

If a train whistle sounds hollow, it is a sign of rain.

        Phyllis Axtell, Lubbock
        Everett Gillis, Lubbock

Worm

If you see some fresh worm mounds, it will rain the next day.

> John Bookman, Canton
> R. W. Maupin, Mabank

MISCELLANEOUS

Acorn

If an old person carries an acorn, his youth will be restored.

> Woodrow Kuhn, Austin
> Larry Taylor, Dallas

Angel

When a conscious silence or lull falls upon a group activity or conversation, an angel is passing overhead.

> Mrs. U. V. Ives, Austin
> Wrenie Evans, Fort Worth

Arrow

Break an arrow in flight and the devil will appear that night.

> F. E. Amos, Amarillo
> Marian Daniel, Denton

Bathing

Latin-American girls should never remove all their clothes when they bathe.

> Esther De La Cruz, Austin
> Barbara Ann Simota, Austin

Beans

If you plant beans while a norther is blowing, they will not cook soft.

> Otto G. Stamman, Temple
> Elaine Stamman, Temple

Bed

If you sleep in the bed of someone that has died, the spirit of the person that died will pull your covers off.

> Herman Sullivan, Carrizo Springs

Beer

Whiskey on beer, have no fear;
Beer on whiskey, very risky.

> Robert Miltner, Dallas

Billfold

When moving into a new house, you should throw your billfold into the house if you wish to have good luck in money matters.

> Wiley Harper, Denton
> Jim Edwards, Denton

Bread

When buttered bread is dropped and falls on the buttered side, you will have bad luck and will be poor.

> Freda Gardner, Port Lavaca
> Mrs. T. A. Carmichael, Port Lavaca

If you drop bread, pick it up and kiss it, and you will never go hungry.

> Mrs. J. B. Pappas, Texarkana
> Betty Ann Pappas, Texarkana

Eating the crust of bread will cause one's hair to grow extremely long and faster than usual.

> Carol Holland, San Antonio
> Florence Lieb, San Antonio

Broom

If you buy a new broom, have it delivered. It is bad luck to move it yourself.

> Mattie Elva Parsley, Fort Worth
> Wynelle Ray, Fort Worth

If you allow someone to hit you with a broom, even in a playful manner, you will be put in jail for a day.

> Mrs. Melvin Baird, Beeville
> Jean Dugat, Beeville

Never move a broom from your old home to your new home, unless you first take three straws from the broom and nail them over the doorway of your old home.

> Herman Sullivan, Carrizo Springs

Cake

When cutting a cake, do not change directions, or you will have bad luck.

> Glenda Burns, Commerce
> James W. Byrd, Dallas

Don't throw away the egg shells until after the cake is baked. It might fall.

> Ray Wood, Raywood

Calendar

It's bad luck to put up a new calendar before the old year is over.

> Bobbie Browder, Dallas
> Judy Ralston, Midlothian

Car

When you see a car with only one headlight, either slap someone or kiss someone.

> Pam Reid, Longview

MISCELLANEOUS

Cement

You'll have good luck if you step on a cement marked Works Progress Administration.

Carol Hulsey, Denton

Chair

You will have bad luck if you turn a chair around on one leg.

Mrs. R. W. Cowley, Santo
Mrs. Tommy T. Thompson, Stephenville

Chicken

Eating a chicken neck will make you pretty.

Mrs. Ollie D. Wilson, Plainview
James W. Wilson, Sanger

Clocks

It is bad luck to have two clocks running in the same room.

Diane Carlock, Port Lavaca
Mrs. T. A. Carmichael, Port Lavaca

Clover

One leaf for fame, one leaf for wealth,
And one leaf for a faithful lover,
And one leaf to bring glorious health,
Are all in a four-leaf clover.

Jerry Fults, Center
Mrs. Vivian Hyer, Center

Coffee

If you drink coffee before you're twelve, you'll turn black.

Cheryl Martin, Gainesville
Don Pope, Gainesville

Conch Shells

Sailors believe it is bad luck to have conch shells in the house.

> Pam Richardson, Matagorda
> Anne Richardson, Bay City

Coyote

My grandfather was "kissed" by a coyote one night while he was sleeping on the front gallery. He said this brought him much good luck.

> Emil Sachtleben, Floresville
> William D. Wittliff, Austin

Creek

Don't cross a creek after dark, or you will have bad luck the next day.

> Charles Baker, Gainesville
> Don Pope, Gainesville

Cross

If you should come upon a place in a pasture where a horse has wallowed, you are supposed to make a cross in the wallowed place with your foot and spit in it or you will have bad luck.

> Mrs. Myrtle Hampton, Bonham
> Mrs. Bernice L. Harris, Lufkin

Crutches

If you walk with crutches when you don't have to, you will be the next person to need them.

> Mrs. David B. Gracy, Austin
> David B. Gracy, Austin

Cucumber

Get a week- (or feeble-) minded person to plant your cucumber seeds, and you'll raise a better crop.

> Mrs. W. C. Cason, Van Alstyne

Devil

If the sun is shining while it is raining, the devil is beating his wife. If you stick a pin in the crack in the sidewalk, you can hear her scream.

>Mrs. Bennach, San Antonio
>Gordon Sutton, San Antonio

If the rain falls while the sun is shining, the devil is beating his wife. Place a needle in the ground and you will hear the commotion.

>Gwendolyn Moore, Dallas
>Elizabeth Washington, Dallas

When a black cat's eyes are large at night, it is because the devil makes them big so the cat can help him do his work.

>Juan Vega, Brownsville
>Pat DeViney, Austin

If you dig further than about a foot into the ground, the devil will reach up, grab the shovel, and pull you in.

>Juan Vega, Brownsville
>Pat DeViney, Austin

At Olmito, Texas, Mr. Schoumann has a "devil's block." They can never get the land level. My brother worked there, and the man told him to level the ground that night, but he didn't tell him it couldn't be leveled. He stopped the tractor to eat something, and something black came and hovered close to him. When he started to hit it with his hat, he couldn't move. It hung around there, and then it left.

>Juan Vega, Brownsville
>Pat DeViney, Austin

Dirt

To get someone to leave town, get three pinches of dirt from a crossroad. Tie them in a new handkerchief, and throw them in a running river while saying the name of the person you want to leave town.

Mrs. Andrea Gomez, Beeville
Jean Dugat, Beeville

Doll

Never sleep with a doll; it will bite you. Some say that it will dance on your head all during the night.

Herman Sullivan, Carrizo Springs

Donkey

If a donkey gets into your house and breaks a table or a chair, you will become a millionaire.

Antonia Corrizales, San Benito
Nicolas Corrizales, San Benito

Eating

Eat different parts of animals and acquire the ability of the animal.

David L. Potter, Poteet
John Igo, San Antonio

Eggs

It is bad luck to put eggs on a bed after you have gathered them.

Mrs. Bertha Reed, Lott
Jean Dugat, Beeville

Evil

If you want to kill evil, find a four-leaf clover and a black widow spider. Take a straight pin and put it through the center of the clover leaf and the head of the spider. When the spider dies, so will present evil die. You cannot kill all evil at one time, but you can kill the evil that is present as a certain time.

Carole Brown, Richardson
Tom Cameron, Denton

Evil Eye

Many people believe in "el ojo" (the evil eye). They believe that if they see or admire some part of another person's clothing or body, they must touch this place or harm will come to that certain person.

Debbie Ewing, San Antonio
Bessie M. Pearce, San Antonio

Evil Spirits

When a person or a child is feared to be in a state of fright or possess an evil spirit, he is taken or goes to an old lady who makes him lie on a bed naked. Then the victim is brushed by a weed of some kind in the form of crosses. The old lady then calls out to the victim, "Come to me, my child; come to me; I am here." If the victim answers, "I am coming, I am coming," he is then cured. This will happen only if he answers willingly.

Tony M. Pedraza, San Antonio
John Igo, San Antonio

To prevent evil spirits from coming into your mouth while yawning, you should cover your mouth with your hand.

Dan Corbin, Austin
Larry Taylor, Dallas

Feathers

Often feathers will form a "crown" or spiral in a feather pillow after many years. If you find one when changing feathers to a new "ticking," it is a bad luck sign.

Mrs. R. C. Joiner, Lake Jackson
Dr. Gladys Polk, Freeport

Fire

When we were picking cotton, sometimes we would sit up until after midnight waiting to see the ball of fire. Every night it would come about two o'clock, and then we would go to sleep. My uncle quit working there because he was afraid of it.

> Juan Vega, Brownsville
> Pat DeViney, Austin

Fish

Do not eat fish when you nurse a baby.

> Sylvia Hazling, Lubbock
> Richard Earnhart, Denton

Eating fish heads will make you smart.

> Frances L. Herring, San Antonio
> Bessie M. Pearce, San Antonio

Flowers

Never steal flowers or a plant from a grave. If you do, the deceased person will curse you. He'll cause you bad luck.

> Mrs. Sophia Perez, Bay City
> Mary Jane Perez, Bay City

Foot

If you put your left foot in your pants before you put in your right one, everything will go wrong all day.

> J. A. Tucker, Wheeler
> L. H. Tucker, Denton

Garlic

Garlic clears a muddled brain.

> Mrs. J. P. Foster, El Paso
> Ann Foster, El Paso

Garlic keeps ghouls away.

>John Averitt, Knox City
>Mrs. Ottis Cash, Knox City

Gas Meter

If you step on a gas meter, you will have bad luck; if you step on a water meter, you will have good luck.

>Barbara Massingill, Hamilton

Gasoline

Add one mothball to ten gallons of gasoline. This will increase power, gas mileage, and performance.

>John K. Coil, Austin

Gasp

If someone is telling you something and gasps and stutters before finishing, the item is untrue and should not be believed.

>Kay Lynne Busbee, Comfort
>Neil Hawkins, Denton

Gold Piece

Bake a one-layer cake and put a gold piece in it. On New Year's Day cut it. The person who gets the slice with the gold piece in it will have good luck all year.

>Angela J. Pappas, Texarkana
>Betty Ann Pappas, Texarkana

Gum

When you chew gum in bed, you are chewing the bones of dead people.

>Herman Sullivan, Carrizo Springs

If you are offered a stick of gum from a newly opened package, choose the middle piece for good luck.

>Sally Harpool, Denton
>David Hendricks, Denton

Gypsies

Gypsies were given a "right to steal" by having stolen one of the nails that would have been used in the crucifixion of Christ.

Jeanne Howard, McKinney

Hair

To comb your hair after dark will bring trouble to your heart.

Mrs. Velma Thompson, Clute

Older people do not want girls to cut their hair. It takes away their modesty.

Ulunda Garcia, Austin
Barbara Ann Simota, Austin

Hands

If you fold your hands across your head, you are locking your troubles in.

Mrs. Janie Boone, Lufkin
Mrs. Bernice L. Harris, Lufkin

Hat

Never let a man lay his hat on a bed with the crown down, or bad sickness will come to the first man who sleeps in the bed.

Mrs. John Stocks, Bluff Dale
Mrs. Tommy T. Thompson, Stephenville

Heels

Wearing down your heels on the outside shows a generous nature. If you wear them down on the inside, you are stingy.

Mrs. Ruby Mann, Houston
Ray Wood, Raywood

Horseshoe

With prongs up a horseshoe will suck the devil in and destroy him if he gets too near. With prongs down, the horseshoe pours out its magic and keeps him from crossing the threshold.

> Jerry Fults, Center
> Mrs. Vivian Hyer, Center

Hotel Register

Never close a hotel register after signing your name, or you will have bad luck.

> Gene Johnson, Dallas
> Larry Taylor, Dallas

Initials

If your first, middle, and last initials are placed in order and form a word, you will be a very rich person. If they do not form a word, you will be poor.

> Roy Whatley, Dallas
> Fleur Fuller, Denton

Invisibility

Evil people who wish to become invisible may boil a black cat in a pot of hot water, take the left leg bones (both front and back), and put them in the mouth behind the two front teeth. This will permit them to be invisible.

> Mrs. De La Cruz, Austin
> Barbara Ann Simota, Austin

Knees

If a boy wears out the knees of his pants, he will be rich some day.

> Mrs. Ruby Mann, Houston
> Ray Wood, Raywood

Knife

If you hand someone back his knife, hand it the way he handed it to you, open or closed, or your friendship will be broken.

> James Cole, Madisonville
> Tommy Batson, Austin

Throw a knife into the whirlwind, and you'll see the devil.

> Mrs. Lemwell East, Austin
> Mrs. Maura Darrouzet, Austin

Laugh

If you laugh at another person's misfortune, then you, too, will have bad luck.

> Mary Ann Nesuda, Dallas
> Larry Taylor, Dallas

Meat

To make soup meat more tender, place the lid of a Mason jar in with the ingredients and cook.

> Gilbert Martinez, Austin
> Frank Rios, Jr., Austin

Mexicans

Mexicans feel that they are of the color brown because God created man by mixing many things in one big pot. He cooked the mixture and first took out white man (not cooked enough), then the Mexican (he was just right), and lastly the Negro (he was overcooked).

> Mrs. Walter Sparks, Jr., Portland
> Gail Mayo, Taft

Milk

Raw milk from cows is all right to drink if it is strained first.

> Mrs. Livia Diaz, Austin
> Barbara Ann Simota, Austin

Milk and lobsters should never be eaten together.

>Nelda Garcia, Austin
>Barbara Ann Simota, Austin

Mirror

If you break a mirror, you will have seven years of bad luck. To break the spell, go to the nearest lake or river and throw the mirror over your shoulder.

>Linda Rai Heath, Athens
>A. C. Norman, Athens

When you break a mirror, you should go to a creek in which the water is running. Then you must close your eyes and drop the pieces into the water.

>Lucille Morris, Jasper
>Colleen Buckley, Beaumont

Mistletoe

Mistletoe was once a beautiful tree with very hard, but easily worked wood. Then the wood from the tree was used to make the cross on which Jesus died. Afterwards the tree shrank to its present day form, a parasite.

>Lela Wyatt, Lufkin
>Jean Dugat, Beeville

Mole

If you have a mole on the right side of the jaw, you will have bad luck.

>Stan McDonald, Austin
>Larry Taylor, Dallas

Money

If a dog with a rattling chain appears, money is hidden where you see the dog.

>Mrs. Andrea Gomez, Beeville
>Jean Dugat, Beeville

A two-dollar bill is considered lucky in the New England states, and in gambling centers, but is considered unlucky in the South unless the upper right-hand corner is clipped off.

>Bullock Hyder, Denton
>D. Michael Frye, Lewisville

If you grow wandering jew in the house, you will never have any money.

>Walter Busby, Dallas

Carrying a penny and a magnet will bring you money.

>Richard Hinojosa, Brownsville
>Pat DeViney, Austin

Moon

It's bad luck to look at the moon when it's orange colored.

>Herman Sullivan, Carrizo Springs

Money made on a moonlit night will in some way do you no good, because as everyone knows the moon smacks of financial ill.

>Howard Hanks, Jr., Denton

Nail

Stepping on a new nail is harmless. Only a rusty nail is dangerous.

>Salvador Vasquez, Austin
>Barbara Ann Simota, Austin

Put a square nail in a pot of beans, cook them, and they will be tender.

>Anna Raye Roach, Gainesville
>Charles R. Horn, Gainesville

Onions

To keep from crying while peeling onions, put a little bit of onion skin (the outer layer) on the top of your head.

> Mrs. C. Spearman, El Paso
> Janet Irvin, El Paso

A piece of onion on the shelf makes the shelf germ free.

> John Mabry, Port Lavaca
> Mrs. T. A. Carmichael, Port Lavaca

Pepper

When you pass the pepper while eating, you should set it down on the table instead of handing it directly to the person. Then the person picks it up. It will bring bad luck if this is not done.

> John David Young, Hamilton

Pepper Plants

Mean people have the best luck with pepper plants.

> Mrs. Lemwell East, Austin
> Mrs. Maura Darrouzet, Austin

If you want your pepper plants to be very hot, plant while you are mad.

> Mrs. Janie Boone, Lufkin
> Mrs. Bernice L. Harris, Lufkin

Petticoat

If you put your petticoat on wrong side out and wear it that way all day, you are all right. If you change it, you'll have bad luck.

> Kathy Hutson, Lubbock
> Mrs. Ralph T. Caldwell, Lubbock

Picture

If you dislike a person and want to harm him in any way, take his picture and bury it face down in the ground. This will also work if you bury his sock under your back porch.

      Mrs. Teresa Flores, San Antonio

Pie

When eating a piece of pie, you must always cut off and eat the tip of the wedge first, or you will have bad luck.

      Loyle McReynolds, Wortham
      Lin Stooksbury, Wortham

Pipe

To take the bite out of a new pipe, fill the bowl full of good whiskey and let it set overnight.

      J. Frank Dobie, Austin
      William D. Wittliff, Austin

Plant

If you thank the giver of a plant (garden plant intended for transplanting), the plant will die.

      Mrs. L. V. Reagan, Denton
      C. H. Neuhaus, Denton

Problem

If you have a problem and want to get rid of it, write it down on a piece of paper and put the paper in the match box. Then bury the box. Don't bury it where you want something to grow, because nothing will grow where the box is buried.

      Merrilee Ann Jones, San Antonio
      John Igo, San Antonio

Railroad Tracks

When you cross the railroad tracks without raising up your feet and singing,
> Railroad, steamboat, river and canal,
> Yonder comes a sucker and he's got my gal,

you will have bad luck.

>> Betty Davis, Knox City
>> Mrs. Ottis Cash, Knox City

Rice

If you stir rice while cooking, a ghost will come and haunt you every night you live.

>> Zellan Jeanne Fitch, Denton
>> Mrs. G. Adams, Denton

Sailor

If a sailor has a pig tattooed on his leg, or a ring of seagulls tatooed on his ankle, he won't drown.

>> Deborah Roemer, Port Lavaca
>> Mrs. T. A. Carmichael, Port Lavaca

Salt

When moving into a new house (before taking your furniture), carry over a small portion of salt, a loaf or a few slices of bread, and a broom. You will never want for food or good fortune.

>> Mrs. Jewell Silber, San Antonio

It is bad luck to pass salt from one person to another. Put the salt shaker on the table and let the other person pick it up.

>> Dean Awalt, Beeville
>> Jean Dugat, Beeville

To burn salt is a sin.

>> Herman Sullivan, Carrizo Springs

Sewing

When you are sewing, and your thread knots or tangles, someone is talking about you.

> Nonie Anderson, Matagorda
> Mrs. Minnie Hatchett, Bay City

Don't ever sew anything on your body unless you put something in your mouth.

> Almarie Chilton, Athens
> A. C. Norman, Athens

Shoe

If you want to get rid of a man, get the sole of his shoe, and tack it to a freight car. The farther away the freight car goes, the farther away from you the man will go.

> Olive Jane Strange, Temple
> Margaret Gresham, Temple

To keep snakes away from your house, burn old shoes of your family's at all four corners.

> Jerry Fults, Center
> Mrs. Vivian Hyer, Center

If your shoes squeak, they are not paid for.

> Mrs. Ruby Mann, Houston
> Ray Wood, Raywood

If your shoe keeps coming untied, someone is thinking of you.

> Bonnie Harris, Sanger
> James Wilson, Sanger

Singing

If you sing unconsciously in the bathtub, it is good luck

> Jerry Fults, Center
> Mrs. Vivian Hyer, Center

MISCELLANEOUS

If you sing in bed at night, you will get up the next morning crying.

> Dave Fowler, Buckholts
> Kerry Fowler, Temple

Singing at the table, whistling in bed,
Boogie-man will get you before you are dead.

> C. E. Allgeier, Denton

Slip

If you put your slip on backwards, you will have good luck.

> Lynn Peiper, Beeville
> Sandy Power, Beeville

Spanish Rice

A heavy iron skillet must be used to make Spanish rice, or it will not turn out right and will taste funny.

> Mrs. Jack W. Clark, El Paso
> Ann Foster, El Paso

Spirits

Churches are haunted by spirits which sing and play the piano at midnight each night. Sometimes the music cannot be heard, but you can see the piano keys going up and down.

> Ulunda Garcia, Austin
> Barbara Ann Simota, Austin

Star

If you see a shooting star falling, open a handkerchief in your hands, and money will come from the sky.

> Gracie Castillo, Cameron
> Avelina Longoria, San Benito

If you count one thousand stars in a single night, you will go crazy.

> Mrs. Cleo Brantner, Bremond
> Jorge Movelos, Jr., Austin

Study

Study your school lesson or memory work, then sleep on the book, and you'll know it all when you awake.

> Tommie Lynn Cade, Dallas
> Gerald B. Pratt, Dallas

Table

Lying on a table is bad luck, as only the dead may lie on a table.

> Amada Canales, Mercedes
> T. M. Harwell, Edinburg

If you sit at the head of a table, it is believed that you are either a minister, a beautiful woman, or a man without shame.

> Rosa Maria C. Ramirez, Laredo
> J. W. Nixon, Laredo

Thorns

Thorns over a door will trap evil.

> Judy Tinker, Houston
> Mrs. Jo Harris, Houston

Tortillas

If you drop tortillas, or they fall, a fat lady is coming to visit you.

> Herman Sullivan, Carrizo Springs

Towel

Towel

Do not dry your hands on opposite ends of a towel at the same time as a friend does, or you will quarrel.

>Alma Diaz, Austin
>Barbara Ann Simota, Austin

Treasure

The ghost of a deceased man may direct his heir to a buried treasure. The heir must go to the treasure at midnight, and no one may substitute for him since he is the rightful owner.

>Tomas Ramirez, Weslaco
>T. M. Harwell, Edinburg

If you find an unusual object in the woods, such as a pile of neatly stacked lumber, and it disappears the next time you look for it, treasure is usually hidden there.

>Manuel Vasquez, Beeville
>Joe Henry Salazar, Beeville

To look for treasure, throw four half dollars into the air. If they fall in the sign of the cross, dig, and you will find the person that had to bury his gold, and he will show you where it is.

>Juan Vega, Brownsville
>Pat DeViney, Austin

Trip

If you are about to drive on a trip, and you announce to all the occupants of the car that you have never had a wreck (and it is true), you will be more likely to have an accident. It will put you on edge.

>Peggy Hendricks, Denton

Trouble

If you laugh a great deal about something, it means that you are going to have some trouble.

Herman Sullivan, Carrizo Srpings

Turnip

If you drop turnip seeds while planting a garden, they'll come up the next day, but the turnips will be rotten.

Billy Tucker, Denver City
Lois Brock, Denver City

Vampires

Vampires and werewolves come out when a full moon goes behind a dark cloud.

John Averitt, Knox City
Mrs. Ottis Cash, Knox City

Walking

If you walk backward, you're cursing your mother.

Linda Rai Heath, Athens
A. C. Norman, Athens

Washing

After washing dishes, you should turn the dishpan slightly on its side, and slowly pour the water out. Leave the dishrag in the pan. If it happens to fall out, then bad luck will soon follow.

Jon Payne, Edna
Grace Wellborn, Lubbock

Wash together, be friends forever; dry together, fight before night.

Thomas B. Mills, Terrell
Linda J. Mills, Terrell

Water

It is a sign of bad luck to spill water on a doorsill.
>Jan Sutton, Knox City
>Mrs. Ottis Cash, Knox City

If you'll put a can of water on a stove that is smoking, it will stop smoking.
>Herman Sullivan, Carrizo Springs

Hot water freezes faster than cold water.
>Gordon E. Parks, Stephenville

When a person asks you for a glass of water, and you don't give it to him, it is bad luck.
>Hilario Segura, Port Lavaca
>Mrs. T. A. Carmichael, Port Lavaca

Watermelon

Place a broom straw on a watermelon. If it begins to turn, the watermelon is ripe.
>J. F. Barron, Denison
>Brent Barron, Irving

Wealth

A small coin placed under the welcome mat in front of a door promises wealth to the first stranger finding it.
>Lewis Dodd, San Antonio
>Bessie M. Pearce, San Antonio

Well

It is bad luck to look in a well.
>Mrs. Lillie Gregg, Athens
>Connie Gregg, Athens

Whistling

Whistling at the table, singing in bed,
The devil will get you before you are dead.

>Linda Hideman, San Antonio

A whistling woman, like a cackling hen,
Will always come to some bad end.

>Sharon Evans, Denton

Willow

A water witch can locate a well by using a willow limb in the shape of a Y. He holds the limb in front with the single prong extended and walks around. When he is over water, the limb will point downward with a definite pull and may even twist around in his hands. Here is the place to dig.

>Clyde Thompson, Whitesboro
>H. D. Odom, Whitesboro

Window

Entering a house through a window brings bad luck. If you enter through a window you must leave through the same window.

>Amada Canales, Mercedes
>Baldemar Zuniga, Mercedes

Wood

If you brag, knock on wood.

>Herman Sullivan, Carrizo Springs

Yam

To grow a yam in the house is bad luck.

>Mariana Guerra, Robstown
>Jan Crain, Austin

INDEX

INDEX

Ability, 78
accident, 27, 61, 93
accompanist, 62
ace, 18, 37, 63, 65
acorn, 72
Adam, 58
adder, 3
adolescent, 45
albino, 33
alum, 55
aluminum, 36
angel, 7, 72
animal(s), 3, 17, 70, 78
ankle, 53, 89
anniversary, 59
announcer, 62
ant, 3, 38, 54, 66
ant bed, 56
apple, 16, 58
apron, 12
area, 48
arena, 65
armadillo, 3, 70
arm pit, 43
arrow, 72
arthritis, 31
ashes, 58
asthma, 31, 32
athlete's foot, 32
August, 57
aunt, 59
avocado tree, 53
ax, 66

Babel, 58
baby, 7, 8, 11, 20, 26, 37, 42, 48, 51, 53, 54, 59, 80
back, 50, 55, 63, 67, 69, 70
back yard, 33
bacon rind, 34
bag, 43, 48, 50, 54
baldness, 32
ball, 64, 80
ball of fire, 80
band, 31
bandage, 53
barbed wire, 40
bark, 31, 38, 40, 57
barn, 44, 51

baseball, 62
basement, 13
bat, 32, 39, 62
batch, 42
bath, 71
bathing, 72
bathtub, 90
batter, 62
beans, 72, 86
bed, 6, 8, 17, 21, 22, 37, 39, 43, 66, 73, 78, 79, 81, 82, 91, 96
bedpost, 8
bedroom, 11
bed wetting, 33
beer, 73
bees, 66
beeswax, 47
Bible, 40, 58
Big Joe's Fishing Camp, 21
bike, 14
bile, 25
billfold, 73
bird, 23, 45
birth, 7, 8
birth pain, 8
bite, 3, 29, 32, 33, 88
black, 23, 24, 37, 39, 45, 55, 62, 75, 77, 78, 83
blackbird, 69
black pepper, 23
black widow spider, 78
bladder, 25
blade, 13
blanket, 51
bleeding, 33
blemish, 34
blister, 34
blood, 4, 23, 34, 37, 39, 41, 56, 58
blood pressure, 34
bloom, 64
blue, 30, 68
bluebonnets, 64
bluing, 3
body, 25, 33, 39, 44, 52, 79, 90
boils, 34, 35
bone, 5, 54, 59, 81, 83
boogie-man, 91
book, 92
boot, 65

bottle, 8, 14, 17, 41
bottom, 19, 21, 38
bowl, 88
bowler, 63
box, 88
boxing, 63
boy, 11, 14, 26, 45, 51
boyfriend, 13, 15, 16, 44
bracelet, 31
brain, 52, 54, 80
Brazos, 63
bread, 15, 37, 40, 73, 89
breath, 12, 18
bride, 11, 15
bridge, 18
bridge game, 18, 63
broom, 74, 89, 95
brother, 50, 77
brown, 30, 33, 35, 53, 84
bruise, 35
bucket, 42, 69
buggy, 50
bull, 3, 4
bump, 6, 56
bundle, 12
bunion, 39
burial, 23
burn, 35, 36
business, 61
butter, 35, 40, 73
butterfly, 18, 23
buttermilk, 45
button, 18
button willow, 38
buzzard, 11, 24, 49

Cabbage, 35, 59
cactus, 36, 47, 67
Cadillac, 14
cake, 74, 81
calendar, 74
calf, 3
callus, 39
can, 56, 58, 94
canal, 89
cancer, 5, 31, 36
candle, 13
candy, 38
capsule, 31

car, 11, 18, 26, 65, 74, 93
card, 18, 63
carrot, 42, 60
cat, 4, 11, 24, 39, 45, 53, 67, 77, 83
caterpillar, 48
cayenne pepper, 47
cement, 75
cemetery, 26, 56
chain, 85
chair, 63, 75, 78
change, 70, 71
charm, 5
check, 6
cheesecloth, 35
cherry, 38
chest, 29, 38, 39
chicken, 4, 13, 36, 45, 48, 56, 57
chicken excrement, 45, 48, 57
chicken neck, 75
chicken pox, 36, 37
Chihuahua dog, 32
child, 8, 10, 32, 41, 54, 79
childhood, 7
child labor, 9
children, 8, 9, 37, 57
chili, 38
chill(s), 27, 43
chimney, 23
chirp, 67
Christ, Jesus, 19, 58, 82, 85
Christmas Eve, 15
church, 91
churning, 71
circle, 28
clasp, 15
clay, 53
cliff, 19
clipping, 44, 68
clock, 42, 75
cloth, 42, 50, 53
clothes, 10, 24, 27, 63, 72, 79
cloud, 66, 94
clover, 75, 78
coach, 63
coal oil, 40, 45
cobweb, 33
coffee, 37, 75
coin, 95
colds, 37, 38

INDEX

color, 18, 35, 50, 84, 86
comb, 27
companion, 12
concert, 62
conch shell, 76
confusion, 58
conjure, 56
consumption, 39
conversation, 72
convertible, 11
cool, 38
coop, 36
copper, 31, 32
cord, 10
corn, 39, 57, 67
cornbread, 54
corner, 9, 11, 55, 86, 90
cornmeal, 42
corpse, 25, 30
cotton, 40, 80
cottonseed, 43
cottonwood, 50
cough, 37, 39
count, 47
couple, 14
courtship, 11
cover, 43, 73
covering, 57
cow, 3, 4, 60, 64, 67, 84
cowardice, 8
cowboy, 65
cowchip, 39, 49
cow manure, 32, 33, 35, 49
cow urine, 49
coyote, 76
crack, 77
cramps, 39
crawl, 24
creek, 76, 85
crick, 39
cricket, 67
crop(s), 57, 61
cross, 19, 52, 76, 79, 85, 93
crossroad(s), 53, 78
crow, 67
crown, 79, 82
crucifixion, 19, 82
crust, 73
crutch, 76

crying, 39
cucumber, 10, 76
cup, 35, 49
cure, 33, 42, 44, 56
curl, 49
curse, 94
cut, 40
cyst, 40

Dallas, 26, 27
dark, 76, 82
date, 18
daughter, 59
day, 6, 8, 11, 13, 18, 19, 21, 22, 26, 28, 31, 32, 34, 40, 42, 46, 55, 57, 58, 60, 64, 66, 68, 70, 72, 74, 76, 80, 87, 94
death, 11, 17, 23, 24, 28, 29, 30, 31, 58
debt, 24
deceased, 80, 93
deer, 31, 33
defect, 9
depth, 21
devil, 6, 72, 77, 83, 84, 96
dew, 45
diarrhea, 40
direction, 74
dirt, 52, 59, 78
dishes, 95
dishpan, 68, 95
dishrag, 95
disinfectant, 4
dog, 4, 5, 25, 33, 51, 52, 55, 60, 85
doll, 78
dominos, 63
donkey, 78
door, 5, 12, 25, 50, 92, 95
doorsill, 94
doorstep, 15
doorway, 74
dream, 17, 21, 22
dress, 16, 18, 19, 26, 38, 61
driver, 65
drop, 15, 38, 41
drouth, 69
drowning, 11, 25, 26
drunkard, 12

Ear, 37, 40, 41, 50, 57, 67
earache, 40

earth, 58
ear wax, 44
east, 25, 61, 64
eating, 78
eclipse, 10
edge, 93
eel, 43
egg, 9, 19, 23, 33, 42, 52, 56, 74, 78
eight, 65
elbow, 56
eleven, 57
embarrassment, 60
emergency, 59
end, 6, 53, 93, 96
enemy, 22, 47
entrance, 12, 65
epilepsy, 41
Eve, 58
evening, 13, 38, 68, 69
evil, 5, 28, 46, 78, 79, 83, 92
evil eye, 25, 79
evil spirits, 79
expulsion, 60
eye, 3, 25, 41, 42, 53, 56, 77, 85
eyelash, 19
eyelid, 19
Ezekiel, 33
Face, 4, 11, 13, 18, 19, 25, 42, 45, 88
family, 17, 23, 24, 25, 27, 28, 29, 31, 90
farmer, 61
father, 41
fear, 73
feather, 4, 28, 68, 79
February, 57
feces, 45
feeble-minded person, 76
feet, 8, 10, 17, 25, 37, 38, 42, 43, 46, 54, 68
female, 4, 12
fence, 40, 67, 69
fertility, 43
fever, 43, 44
fever blister, 44
fifteen, 67
fig leaves, 50, 51
fig tree, 35
financial loss, 61, 86
finger, 14, 20, 41, 47, 66
fingernail(s), 10, 44

fire, 3, 4, 28, 32, 52, 80
first, 65
fish, 5, 20, 23, 26, 50, 64, 80
fishing, 64
fits, 41, 44
five, 35, 47, 58
flag, 64
flight, 72
flood, 58
floor, 17, 35, 61
flowers, 56, 80
folk medicine, 31
food, 7, 89
fool, 53
foot, 6, 7, 22, 36, 40, 60, 76, 80
football, 64
footsteps, 46
forefinger, 48
forehead, 47
forewarning, 22
fork, 4, 20, 68
form, 85
fortune, 89
forty, 67
four, 16, 18, 26, 42, 56, 59, 63, 75, 78, 90, 93
four-leaf clover, 78
fourteenth, 57
freckle(s), 45
freight car, 90
Friday, 6, 58
friend, 6, 19, 24, 50, 93, 95
friendship, 84
fright, 79
frog, 6, 44, 68
front, 95, 96
fruit crop, 57
frying pan, 12
funeral, 26
fungus, 32
furniture, 89

Gall bladder, 25
gallery, 76
gambling center, 86
game, 62, 63, 65, 66
garden, 88, 94
gargle, 45
garlic, 34, 40, 80, 81

INDEX

garment, 58
gases, 69
gas meter, 81
gasoline, 81
gasp, 81
germ, 87
ghost, 26, 89, 93
ghoul, 81
gift, 62
girl, 12, 14, 15, 26, 38, 51, 59, 82, 89
girlfriend, 44
giver, 88
glass, 17, 95
goal, 64
goat pills, 43
God, 84
gold, 59, 81, 93
gold pin, 56
golf, 64
Good Friday, 58
Gordonville, 21
grasshopper, 5, 45
grave, 20, 25, 27, 30, 47, 56, 80
graveyard, 12, 20
gray, 68, 69
grazing, 64
grease, 39, 49, 53
green, 13, 65
green peas, 59
ground, 9, 21, 33, 57, 60, 66, 68, 77, 88
group, 72
gum, 20, 50, 54, 59, 81
gypsies, 82

Hail, 68
hailstone, 68
hair, 9, 10, 12, 27, 32, 45, 46, 49, 50, 59, 61, 73, 82
haircut, 45
half, 41, 54, 58
half dollar, 93
Halloween, 13
hand, 3, 13, 14, 16, 41, 43, 53, 56, 63, 79, 82, 91, 93, 96
handkerchief, 9, 13, 63, 78, 91
hangover, 46
harm, 46, 79
hat, 22, 55, 77, 82
hatband, 52

haunt, 89
hawk, 8
hay fever, 46
head, 5, 9, 10, 18, 28, 32, 35, 36, 37, 43, 44, 46, 48, 52, 54, 61, 64, 66, 69, 78, 82, 87, 92
headache, 46, 47
headlight, 74
health, 47
heart, 8, 13, 39, 47, 82
hearth, 67
heaven, 30
heel, 8, 39, 82
heir, 93
hem, 19
hen, 9, 96
hex, 44
hiccoughs, 47, 48
hickory, 40
highway, 71
hill, 65, 70
hit, 62
hive, 66
hives, 48
hog, 39, 47, 68
hole, 3, 32, 56, 64, 66
holy water, 32
home, 5, 10, 23, 24, 74
honey, 31, 37, 43
honeybee, 48
honeycomb, 46
horehound tea, 37
horn, 31
horned toad, 6, 30
horse, 6, 20, 56, 76
horse manure, 56
horseshoe, 83
hotel register, 83
hour, 12, 42, 52, 70
house, 3, 6, 7, 9, 16, 17, 23, 24, 25, 26, 27, 30, 31, 73, 76, 78, 86, 89, 90, 96
huevo de torro, 46
human body, 31
hundred, 20
hunting, 65
husband, 13, 14, 15, 16, 17
Illness, 48
inch, 60
Indian, 19

infancy, 7
infection, 40
ingredients, 84
initial(s), 13, 14, 83
intelligence, 9, 46
invisibility, 83
iodine, 38
iron, 13, 32, 49, 91
itch, 48
item, 81

Jail, 74
jalapeño pepper, 38
jar, 31, 60, 84
jaw, 85
jaybird, 6
jigger, 23
jinx, 64
juice, 41, 47, 51, 52, 67
July 30th, 58
jump, 27

Kerosene, 33
key, 10, 50
kidney, 49
kildeer, 70
killer, 29
kin, 24
kiss, 14, 15, 19, 73, 74, 76
kissing, 18
kitchen, 14
knee, 5, 56, 83
knife, 8, 9, 14, 33, 52, 84
knothole, 60

Labor, 9
lady, 79, 92
lake, 21, 26, 85
Lake Texoma, 21
lamp, 27, 40
land, 77
lard, 40, 47
Latin-American girls, 72
laugh, 84, 94
laundry, 12
leaf(ves), 35, 42, 43, 50, 57, 75
left, 62, 80, 83
leg, 39, 40, 62, 75, 83, 89
legend, 26

lemon, 7, 34
lemonade, 37
lesson, 92
letter, 14
lid, 84
lie, 19, 44
life, 11, 17, 28, 54
light, 7, 18
lightning, 68, 71
lily, 43
limb, 49
line, 10
lineman, 61
liniment, 47
linseed oil, 36
lion, 20
lizard, 6
loaf, 89
lobsters, 85
Lord's Prayer, 48
love, 11, 12, 13, 16
lover, 11
luck, bad, 12, 17, 21, 22, 26, 58, 63, 65, 73, 74, 75, 76, 78, 79, 80, 81, 83, 84, 85, 86, 87, 88, 89, 92, 94, 95, 96
luck, good, 16, 19, 59, 62, 63, 64, 65, 73, 75, 76, 81, 86, 89, 91
lull, 72
lye soap, 35

Madstone, 33
magic, 18, 59, 83
magnet, 86
maid, 15, 56
maiden name, 14
major leaguers, 62
malaria, 49
mal de ojo, 25, 79
male, 4
manufacturer, 61
manure, 32, 51, 56
mark, 32, 44
marriage, 11, 14, 59
Mason jar, 84
master, 27
match, 39, 41, 63
match box, 88
mattress, 9

INDEX

May, 58
May Day, 13, 58
May first, 14, 45
meal, 15
measles, 49
meat, 63, 84
medicine, 57
memory, 21, 92
menstruation, 49
meter, 81
Mexican, 26, 84
Mexican hairless dog, 51
middle, 20, 56, 81
midnight, 29, 45, 80, 91, 93
mildew, 37
mileage, 81
milk, 4, 51, 60, 71, 84
millionaire, 78
mind, 24, 41
minister, 92
minute, 35, 41, 42, 48
mirror, 13, 15, 26, 66, 85
misfortune, 84
mistletoe, 85
mix, 45
mixture, 31, 38, 41, 42, 43, 84
modesty, 82
moisture, 42
molasses, 35, 36
mole, 85
money, 5, 21, 73, 85, 86, 91
moon, 7, 9, 15, 21, 64, 69, 86, 94
morning, 4, 11, 32, 56, 68, 69, 91
mosquito, 39
mothball, 81
mother, 7, 8, 10, 27, 30, 36, 52, 54, 94
mound, 72
mountain, 21
mouse, 54
mouth, 14, 39, 44, 46, 50, 54, 59, 68, 79, 83, 90
mud, 22, 39
mule, 20
mullen tea, 37
mumps, 50
murder, 29
mushrooms, 32
music, 91
musical instrument, 71

musician, 62
mustache, 50
mustard, 8

Nail, 43, 55, 74, 82, 86
name, 11, 12, 13, 14, 16, 78, 83
nature, generous, 82
navel, 7
neck, 7, 10, 15, 32, 38, 39, 50, 54, 55, 75
needle, 77
Negro, 56, 84
nest, 45
net, 65
New England, 86
New Year's Day, 59, 81
next of kin, 24
night, 5, 6, 10, 16, 17, 20, 21, 22, 26, 32, 39, 43, 46, 56, 59, 70, 72, 76, 77, 78, 80, 86, 89, 91, 92, 95
nine, 17, 24, 54
no-hitter, 62
north, 44, 57, 64
norther, 68, 69, 70
nose, 10
nosebleed, 50
number(s), 17, 26, 44, 57, 62, 64
nursing, 7, 80

Oak stump, 34
oil, 38, 39, 41
ojo, el, 79
okra, 69
old maid, 15
Olmito, Texas, 77
one, 18, 43, 46, 57, 62, 68, 74, 75, 79
onion, 35, 37, 38, 39, 41, 43, 55, 69, 87
opium, 44
orange, 7, 86
owl, 6, 7, 28

Pack, 20
"Padoodalie", 18
pain, 8, 9, 36, 52, 54
paint, 58
pair, 53, 65
paisano, 47
palm, 14, 43
pan, 12, 95
pants, 80, 83

paper, 12, 16, 27, 50, 53, 88
parsley, 34
pasture, 67, 76
patient, 43, 44, 51
paw, 67
peace, 24
pear tree, 15
peas, 59
peccary, 4
Pekinese, 5
pellagra, 31
pendant, 15
penny, 51, 62, 86
pepper, 23, 38, 46, 47, 61, 87
petticoat, 87
piano, 71, 91
piano keys, 91
picking cotton, 80
picture, 28, 88
pie, 21, 88
pig, 89
pile, 93
pillow, 28, 68, 79
pin, 56, 77, 78
pinch, 78
pine tar, 31
pint jar, 31
pipe, 21, 39, 88
pitcher, 62
plant, 88
plastic, 48
plate, 29
player, 18, 62, 63
plum, 31
pneumonia, 51
pocket, 7, 21
pod, 40, 69
poison, 33
pokeberry, 48
poker, 65
pole, 61
porch, 24, 88
portent, 29
possession, 44
possum, 27
post, 57, 68
pot, 12, 55, 83, 84, 86
potato, 30, 36, 37
poultice, 34, 35, 43, 53
power, 59, 81

prayer, 52
pregnancy, 10, 51
prickly pear, 34
Prince Charming, 20
professions, 61
profit, 61
prong, 83, 96
Psalms, 24
pumpkin, 49
putt, 64

Quail, 28
quarrel, 14, 15, 19
quarter, 55
queen, 37
quinine, 46

Rabbit, 7, 54, 63, 65, 70
raccoon, 70
racing, 65
radio, 27
rafter, 3
rag, 43
railroad, 89
railroad tracks, 89
rain, 23, 32, 56, 66, 67, 68, 69, 70, 71, 72, 77
rainstorm, 66
raisin, 31
rat, 7, 29, 33
rattler, 55
rattlesnake, 39, 41, 55
red, 37, 46, 53, 68, 69
red ant, 54
red onion, 37
red pepper, 46, 61
retailing business, 61
rheumatism, 51
rhubarb, 46
rhyme, 14, 53
ribbon cane syrup, 38
rice, 89, 91
ride, 65
rider, 65
right, 62, 63, 80, 85, 86
"right to steal", 82
ring, 17, 28, 51, 89
ringworm, 51
river, 78, 85, 89
roadrunner, 35, 47

INDEX

rock, 52
rodeo, 65
roof, 18
room, 12, 55, 59, 75
rooster, 29
root, 31, 38, 48
rope, 65
rosin, 47
row, 27, 56
running, 52
rupture, 25
rusty nail, 86

Sack, 41
sailor, 76, 89
St. John's Day, 59
saliva, 48, 51, 55
salt, 28, 41, 44, 89
salve, 35
sand, 42
sap, 40
sassafras oil, 47
sassafras tea, 34
Saturday, 59
saucer, 29
school, 92
score, 63
scorpion, 70
scrap, 50
scraping, 35
sea, 25, 29, 42
sea gull, 89
season(s), 46, 57
second, 65
seed, 49, 57, 61, 69, 76, 94
seller, 61
seven, 85
seventh, 59
sewing, 60, 90
shadow, 24
shaker, 89
shame, 92
shark, 25, 70
shavings, 53
sheet, 52
shell, 33, 56, 74
shirt, 13
shoe, 5, 6, 15, 18, 21, 22, 29, 39, 46, 48, 90
shoelace, 62

shoulder, 13, 52, 85
shovel, 77
shuck, 67
sickness, 82
side, 19, 44, 50, 73, 85, 95
side pain, 52
sidewalk, 77
sign, 12, 14, 20, 30, 52, 67, 68, 69, 71, 93, 94
signature, 12
silence, 72
silk, 9
silkweed, 31
silver, 21, 28
sin, 89
singing, 16, 71, 90, 91, 96
skillet, 91
skin, 37, 39, 45, 69, 87
skunk, 38, 70
sky, 91
slap, 74
sleep, 39, 43, 52, 61, 73, 78, 80, 82, 92
sleeping, 32, 46, 76
slice, 81, 89
slip, 91
smallpox, 52
smoke, 4, 41
smoking, 39, 94
snake, 7, 22, 29, 44, 90
snow, 60
soap, 35, 53
sock, 88
soda, 36
sole, 43, 90
soot, 33
sore, 6, 34, 37, 52, 54
soul, 24, 30
soup, 55, 84
south, 64, 86
southeast, 70
sow bugs, 54
Spanish rice, 91
spasms, 53
spell, 85
spider, 16, 29, 40, 44, 78, 79
spiral, 79
spirit(s), 28, 37, 73, 91
spit, 48, 52, 76
splinter, 53
spoon, 41

spoonful, 44
sports, 62
spot, 21, 26
sprained ankle, 53
spread, 25
spring, 34
squirrel, 57
stage, 62
stairway, 17
star, 30, 91, 92
staurolite crystal, 19
steamboat, 89
step, 5, 13, 15
stick, 20, 68, 81
sticker, 67
stink, 42
stocking, 62
stomach, 3, 25, 36, 43, 51
stomach-ache, 53
stone, 19, 33
stone bruise, 35
story, 26
stove, 41, 94
stranger, 95
straw, 74, 95
street, 56
strike, 63
string, 10, 38, 40, 63
strip, 16
study, 92
stump, 34, 45
stutter, 81
sty, 53, 59
succession, 48, 60
sucker, 89
sugar, 7, 12, 33, 35, 37, 53
suit, 18, 62
sun, 25, 30, 77
Sunday, 60
sundown, 29, 30, 34
sunrise, 56
surface, 53
sweeping, 16, 59
sweet gum tree, 32
sweetheart, 11, 16
sweet potato, 30
syrup, 31, 38
system, 33

Table, 16, 78, 87, 91, 92, 96

tablespoon, 35
tail, 4, 5, 7, 13, 53, 67, 70
tale, 21
tape, 53
tar, 31, 50
tarantula, 71
taste, 44
tattoo, 25, 89
tea, 31, 33, 34, 37, 38, 43, 48, 49, 53
tears, 19, 22
teaspoon, 53
teaspoonful, 55
teeth, 50, 53, 83
teething, 54
telephone wire, 71
temperature, 67
ten, 20, 23, 35, 47, 81
tennis, 65
terrapin, 71
Texas, 5
thimble, 60
thirteen, 54, 69
thirty, 28
thorn, 47, 92
thousand, 92
thrash (thrush), 54, 59
thread, 51, 90
three, 15, 18, 26, 27, 28, 31, 40, 42, 46, 48, 55, 56, 60, 63, 66, 68, 70, 74, 78
threshold, 59, 83
throat, 37, 38, 50, 54
thunder, 71
thunderstorm, 71
"ticking", 79
time(s), 11, 12, 15, 19, 20, 26, 27, 28, 31, 48, 55, 57, 59, 60, 66, 79, 93
tip, 5, 88
tobacco, 41
toe, 22, 43, 48
toenail, 44, 60
tomato, 54
tomorrow, 67
tongue, 3, 6, 47, 66
tonsil, 55
toothache, 55
tooth decay, 55
top, 41
tortilla, 92
touch, 79
towel, 93

INDEX

tower, 58
town, 56, 78
track(s), 47, 89
tractor, 77
trades, 61
trail, 7
train, 71
traveler, 69
treasure, 93
treatment, 49
tree, 15, 32, 39, 40, 45, 57, 85
triangle, 21
trick, 18, 63
trip, 20, 29, 93
trouble(s), 28, 54, 82, 94
trousers, 8, 53
tuberculosis, 31, 55
Tupelo, Mississippi, 56
turnip, 94
turpentine, 37, 38
twelve, 21, 75
twenty-four, 52, 70
twig, 32
two, 18, 31, 35, 37, 38, 42, 43, 47, 56, 63, 68, 75, 80, 83
two-dollar bill, 86
typhoid, 55
Ulcer, 55
umbilical cord, 11
umbrella plant, 70
uncle, 80
upstairs, 8
urinating, 56
urine, 49
user, 29
utility pole, 61

Vampire, 94
vanilla extract, 36
variation, 44
veil, 11
verse, 24
version, 18
vessel, 28
victim, 79
vine, 30, 42
vinegar, 43, 53
Virginia Fairy Cross, 19
volleyball, 66

Wacoan, 63
walking, 22, 94
walnuts, 51
wandering jew, 86
warning, 17
wart, 56, 59
wash, 62, 95
washpot, 41
water, 12, 21, 22, 27, 32, 34, 38, 41, 42, 43, 45, 48, 52, 53, 54, 55, 56, 57, 60, 69, 70, 71, 83, 85, 94, 95, 96
watermelon, 42, 49, 52, 95
water meter, 81
water witch, 96
wax, 44
way, 69
wealth, 95
weather, 66, 69, 70, 71
web, 44
wedding, 11, 12, 15, 16
wedding dress, 16
wedding ring, 17, 51, 59
wedge, 88
weed, 38, 46, 79
week, 6, 31, 56
weekend, 56
welcome mat, 95
well, 14, 17, 21, 95, 96
werewolf, 94
west, 61, 64
wharf rat, 33
wheat, 13
wheat bran, 42
wheel, 50
whippoorwill, 30
whirlwind, 70, 84
whiskey, 23, 31, 37, 38, 73, 88
whistle, 60, 71, 91, 96
white, 13, 20, 26, 35, 42, 44, 48, 62, 84
White Rock Lake, 26
wife, 7, 41, 77
willow limb, 96
wind, 57, 64
window, 13, 17, 24, 30, 96
wine, 44
wing, 11
winning streak, 62, 63
winter, 60, 66, 67, 69
wire, 31, 32, 40
wisdom teeth, 54

wish, 17, 18, 19, 21, 63
witchcraft, 59
wolf, 43
wood, 85, 96
woodpecker, 31
woods, 32, 93
word, 18, 83
work, 92
Works Progress Administration, 75
world, 8
worm(s), 57, 72
wound, 4, 32, 33, 35, 53, 57

wreath, 28
wreck, 93
wrinkle, 13
wrist, 31

"Y", 96
yam, 96
yard, 33, 60
yawning, 79
year, 21, 25, 56, 59, 74, 79, 81, 85
yerba de la víbora, 38
youth, 72

13.88

398
HEN   Hendricks, George D.
         Mirrors, mice and mustaches.

		DATE DUE		

GRADY MIDDLE SCHOOL LIBRARY